From Your Friends At **The MAILBOX®**

OCTOBER

A MONTH OF REPRODUCIBLES AT YOUR FINGERTIPS!

Kindergarten

Editors:
Ada Goren
Angie Kutzer

Writers:
Joe Appleton, Susan Bunyan, Susan DeRiso, Diane Gilliam,
Lucia Kemp Henry, Katie Padilla, Kelli Plaxco

Art Coordinator:
Clevell Harris

Artists:
Cathy Spangler Bruce, Pam Crane, Nick Greenwood,
Lucia Kemp Henry, Susan Hodnett, Sheila Krill,
Kimberly Richard, Rebecca Saunders, Donna K. Teal

Cover Artist:
Jennifer Tipton Bennett

www.themailbox.com

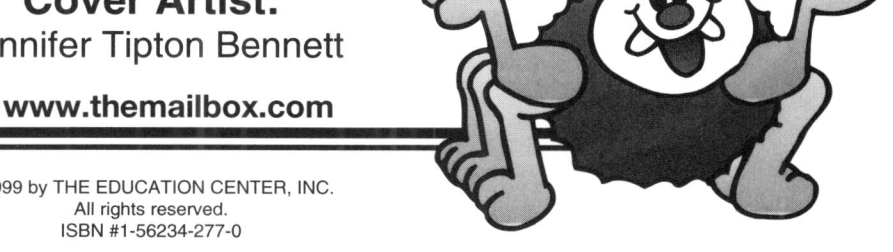

©1999 by THE EDUCATION CENTER, INC.
All rights reserved.
ISBN #1-56234-277-0

Except as provided for herein, no part of this publication may be reproduced or transmitted in any form or by any means, electronic or mechanical, including photocopying, recording, or storing in any information storage and retrieval system or electronic online bulletin board, without prior written permission from The Education Center, Inc. Permission is given to the original purchaser to reproduce patterns and reproducibles for individual classroom use only and not for resale or distribution. Reproduction for an entire school or school system is prohibited. Please direct written inquiries to The Education Center, Inc., P.O. Box 9753, Greensboro, NC 27429-0753. The Education Center®, *The Mailbox®,* and the mailbox/post/grass logo are registered trademarks of The Education Center, Inc. All other brand or product names are trademarks or registered trademarks of their respective companies.

Manufactured in the United States
10 9 8 7 6 5 4 3 2

Table Of Contents

October Planner 3
Organize your monthly themes, special occasions, books and materials, and classroom activities on this form.

October Record Sheet 4
Check out this handy monthly checklist form.

Pass The Pizza! 5
Celebrate National Pizza Month with these spicy ideas!

Pasta Possibilities 11
Spaghetti, rotini, macaroni, too.
Noodles are great teaching tools for you!

Get Poppin'! 19
Popcorn isn't just fun and crunchy—it's educational.

Fire Prevention Week 23
Get youngsters fired up about fire safety!

All In The Family 27
Want great activities about families? They're "relative-ly" easy to find. Look here!

'Tis The Season For...Leaves! 31
Jump into this pile of autumn-leaf ideas.

In The Pumpkin Patch 37
These pages are the pick of the patch!

Spiffy Spiders 43
These eight-legged critters will have little ones spinning with delight!

Happy Halloween! 49
This "boo-tiful" booklet focuses on the colors of Halloween.

It's Nighttime! 57
Break out your bunny slippers and let's get ready for bed!

OCTOBER

PASS THE PIZZA!

Mmmm…gooey cheese, spicy sauce, and crunchy crust. What could be better than pizza? Invite your youngsters to slice into these fun activities centered around this favorite food.

I'll have a large Supreme, please!

At The Pizza Shop

Transform your dramatic-play area into a pizza restaurant! Arrange the furniture to resemble a kitchen area and a dining area. Add bowls, utensils, pizza pans, a telephone, pads and pencils, a toy cash register, and a few pizza boxes (donated by a friendly local pizza place). Gather three sizes of cardboard pizza rounds, cake rounds, or circles cut from sturdy tagboard for little ones to use in making pretend pizzas. Cut appropriately sized circles of red construction-paper sauce to top the three sizes of crusts. Cut some yellow yarn into small pieces to serve as cheese.

Then use the reproducibles on pages 7–9 to add to the fun!

- Duplicate a few copies of the toppings on page 7 onto white construction paper. Color the toppings; then laminate them before cutting them out. Place these in the kitchen for young chefs to use in preparing pizzas.
- Duplicate a supply of the menu/order sheet on page 8. Color a few copies; then laminate them. Have a host or hostess hand these menus to customers. Clip the uncolored copies on clipboards, and have waiters and waitresses use them to mark customers' orders.
- Duplicate one copy of the recipe cards on page 9. Color the cards; then laminate them and post them in your kitchen for little chefs to follow as they create made-to-order pizzas.

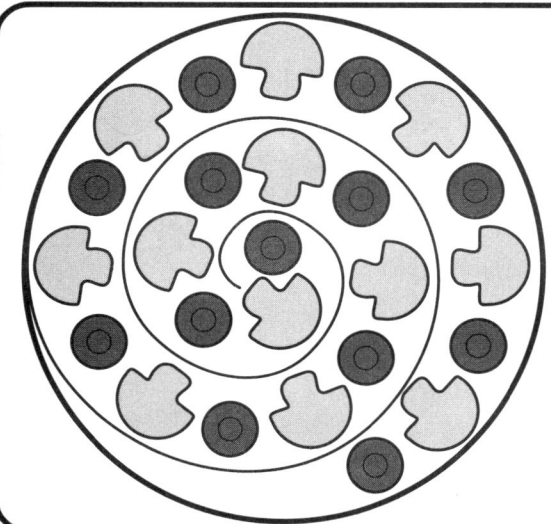

Tip-Top Toppings

Peppers and olives and mushrooms, oh my! Use the topping patterns on page 7 for patterning practice. Invite youngsters to color and cut out the toppings, then glue them in a pattern on a sentence strip. Or, for more of a challenge, have a child lay out her pattern in a spiral beginning at the outer edge of a pizza circle and ending in the center. Invite youngsters to make these pizzas "to go"—home, that is! Encourage youngsters to take home their finished patterning projects and share their knowledge of patterns with their families.

ALL SET FOR PEPPERONI

Use a popular pizza topping to help youngsters practice making sets from one to ten. Duplicate a class supply of page 10. Direct each student to color the pizza. Then have her look at the numeral on each slice and draw the corresponding number of pepperoni rounds. As a variation, duplicate the page onto white construction paper for each child. Have students glue on sets of cinnamon red hots to represent pepperoni slices.

SMALL, MEDIUM, OR LARGE?

The answer to that question is an important part of any pizza order—and an important sorting skill, too! Set up a size-sorting center with the help of a local pizza restaurant. Ask for three pizza boxes: one small, one medium, and one large. Then gather an assortment of items that are available in three distinct sizes, such as spoons, gift bags, books, plastic containers, and blocks. Place the boxes and items in a center. Students visiting this center sort the items by size, then deliver the boxes to the teacher for checking.

PYRAMID PIZZA

The ingredients in this pizza make for a luscious lesson on the Food Guide Pyramid. In advance, prepare your favorite pizza crust recipe. Have a picture of the Food Guide Pyramid on display for reference. Then build the pizza as youngsters watch. Use the directions below when pointing out the ingredients from each section of the Food Guide Pyramid. When it's assembled, bake the pizza and then invite your students to gobble up this nutritious, delicious lesson!

Grain—Start with the crust of the pizza, from the grain section of the pyramid. That's the biggest section of the pyramid, so the crust is the biggest part of the pizza.

Vegetables—Add lots of tomato sauce, as well as chopped green pepper and onion.

Fruits—Drain a small can of pineapple tidbits; then add them to the pizza.

Dairy—Add cheese, but not as much as you may be accustomed to. Remember, we're getting closer to the top of the pyramid!

Meat/Protein—Add some fully cooked low-fat ham. It's more healthful than pepperoni or sausage.

Sugar/Fat—Don't add anything from this section of the pyramid. Remember, this is the smallest section of the pyramid, and we should eat these foods infrequently.

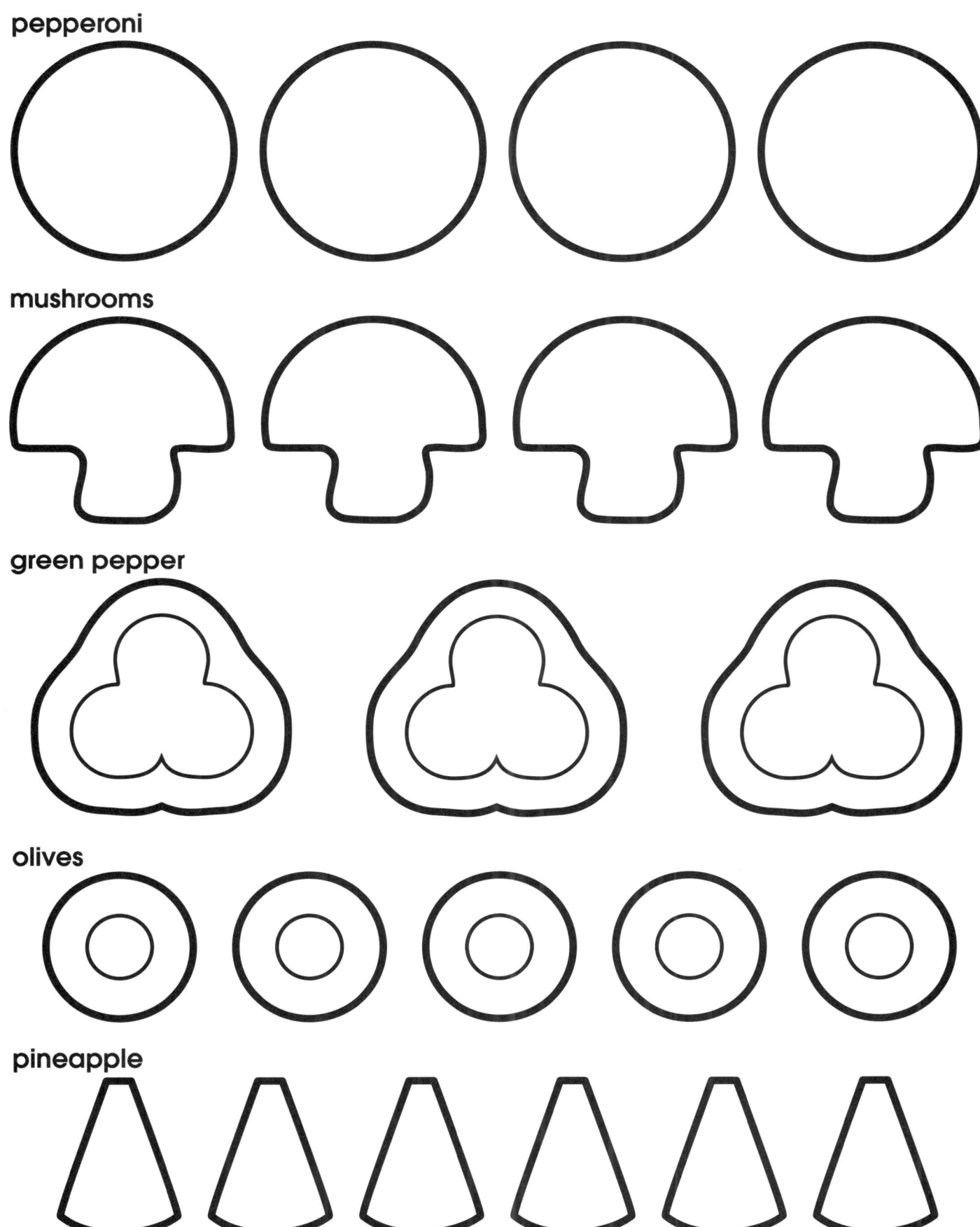

Menu/Order Sheet
Use with "At The Pizza Shop" on page 5.

Pizza Recipe Cards
Use with "At The Pizza Shop" on page 5.

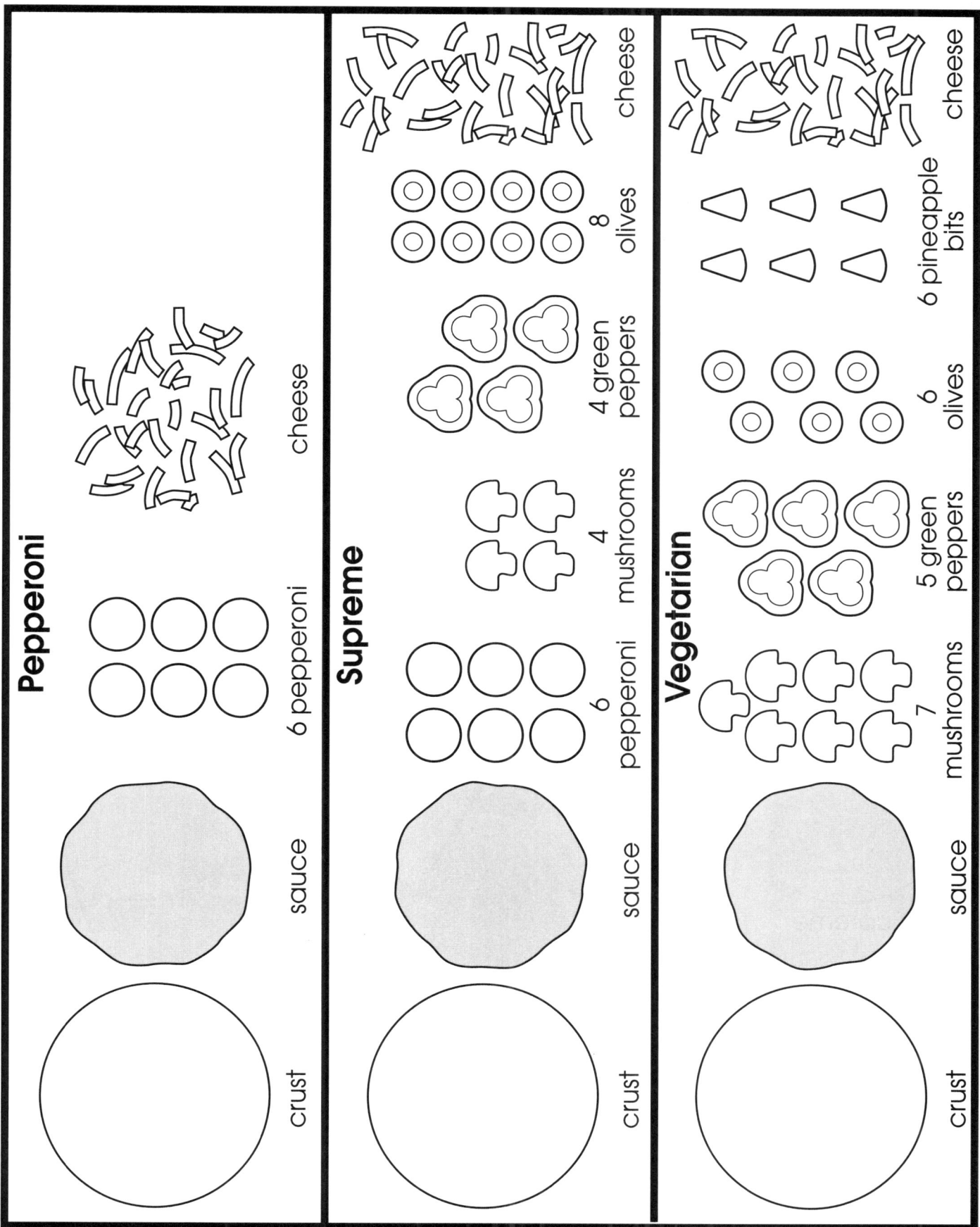

Make Mine Pepperoni!

Name_____

Read the numeral.
Make a set to match.

- 6
- 4
- 10
- 3
- 5
- 8

Pasta Possibilities

Get your students using their noodles with oodles of reproducibles just right for the month of October—National Pasta Month!

Spaghetti Sequencing

Whip up some spaghetti and sauce for a special snack during your pasta unit. Then follow up with the sequencing reproducible on page 13. Give a copy of the page to each child and discuss what is shown in each picture. Ask each child to color her four pictures and cut them out. Provide each student with a 6" x 18" strip of construction paper on which to glue her pictures in sequence from left to right.

Guess The Noodle

Pasta comes in a multitude of shapes. Get youngsters thinking carefully about the differences between various types of pasta with the reproducible on page 14. To prepare, give each child a copy of page 14, glue, and one piece of each of the following: spaghetti, fettucine, rotini, rigatoni, and elbow macaroni. (All the pasta should be uncooked.) Read aloud each description and ask students to determine which noodle the statement describes. Have each child glue her chosen noodle in place below the statement. Short, curvy, not-so-fat—do you see a noodle that looks like that?

All Sorts Of Pasta

The great variety of pasta makes it a perfect manipulative for sorting. Set up a pasta-sorting center with a big pot of mixed, dried pasta and several paper plates, each labeled with a picture of a different type of pasta. Invite youngsters to sort the pasta from the pot onto the corresponding plates. For more pasta-sorting fun, give each child a copy of page 15. Have each student cut out the boxes at the bottom of the page and glue the pasta shapes onto the corresponding plates. As a variation, provide real pasta shells, elbow macaroni, and wagon-wheel pasta for students to sort onto their papers.

Count On Pasta

Noodles make "pasta-tively" wonderful math manipulatives! Provide wagon wheels, shells, corkscrews, or rigatoni, and help your little ones practice counting and creating sets up to ten with these fun counters. Then give each child a copy of page 16 to assess her counting skills. Encourage each child to count the pictured pasta in each box and circle the correct numeral below the set.

Pasta Dominoes

A game of dominoes builds skills with counting and visual matching. Develop those same skills with this thematic version of that favorite game. Duplicate the pasta dominoes on pages 17 and 18 on sturdy tagboard; then cut out all the cards. Laminate them for durability. Have a pair or small group play the game dominoes-style. Ask players to match either the type of pasta on the domino that's played (elbow macaroni to elbow macaroni) or both the type of pasta and the actual number shown on the domino that's played (five wagon wheels to five wagon wheels). Count, match, and learn!

Silly Spaghetti

Youngsters will chuckle when they show off this look-alike spaghetti to their moms and dads. To make a plate of silly spaghetti, each child will need:

— a small paper plate
— glue
— several long lengths of white (or off-white) yarn
— a few small brown pom-poms
— a plastic spoon
— Spaghetti Sauce Paint (see box)
— garlic powder
— a plastic fork

Directions:
1. Squirt glue over the paper plate.
2. Arrange yarn lengths to resemble spaghetti noodles.
3. Glue a few pom-pom meatballs in place on top of the noodles.
4. Spoon some Spaghetti Sauce Paint over the spaghetti and meatballs.
5. Sprinkle some garlic powder over the paint (to resemble cheese).
6. Stick a plastic fork into the spaghetti.
7. Let the whole project dry thoroughly.

Spaghetti Sauce Paint
3 parts red tempera paint
1 part brown tempera paint
1 part white glue
a few sprinkles of basil

Sequencing Cards
Use with "Spaghetti Sequencing" on page 11.

Name _____

Pasta Possibilities
Critical thinking

Noodle Riddles

Listen.
Think.
 Glue.

1. This noodle is long and round.

2. This noodle is short and twisted.

3. This noodle has ridges. You can see through it.

4. This noodle is long and flat.

5. This noodle is short and curved.

Name _____

Pasta Possibilities
Sorting

A Pasta Assortment

©1999 The Education Center, Inc. • *October Monthly Reproducibles* • Kindergarten • TEC959

15

Name _____

Oodles Of Noodles

Pasta Possibilities
Counting

Count the pasta in each box.
Circle the correct numeral.

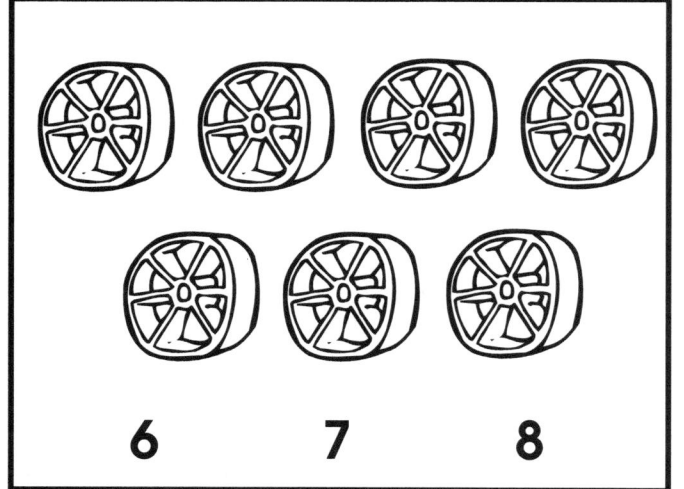
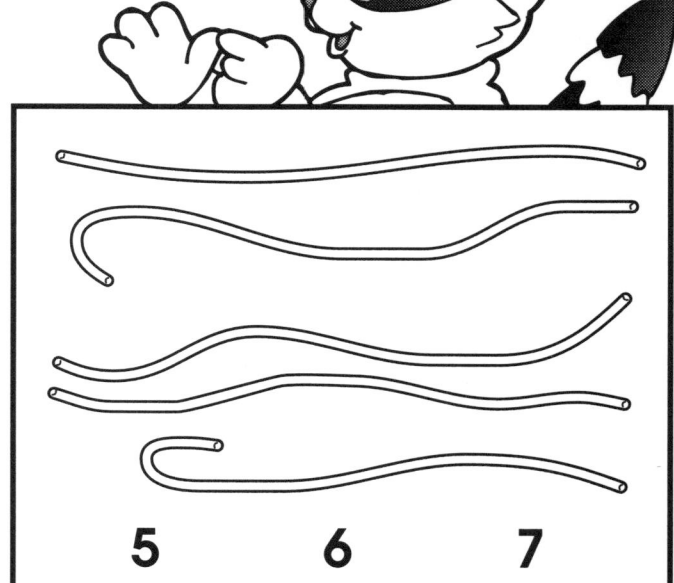
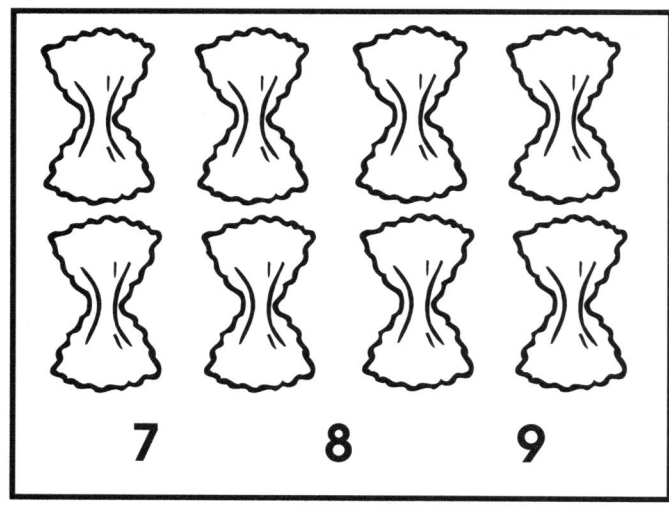
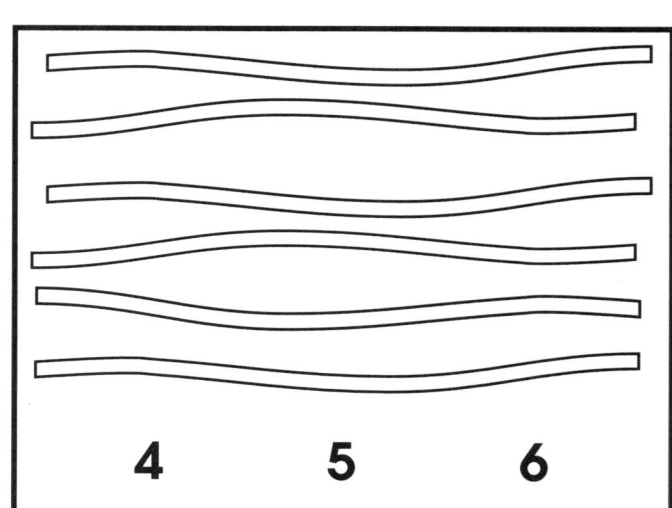
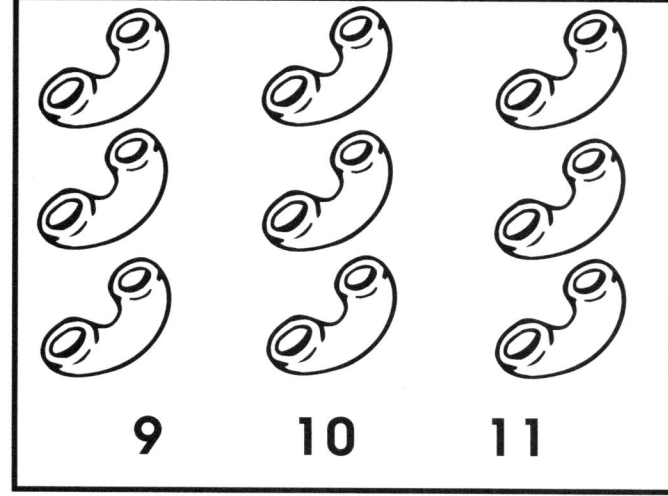
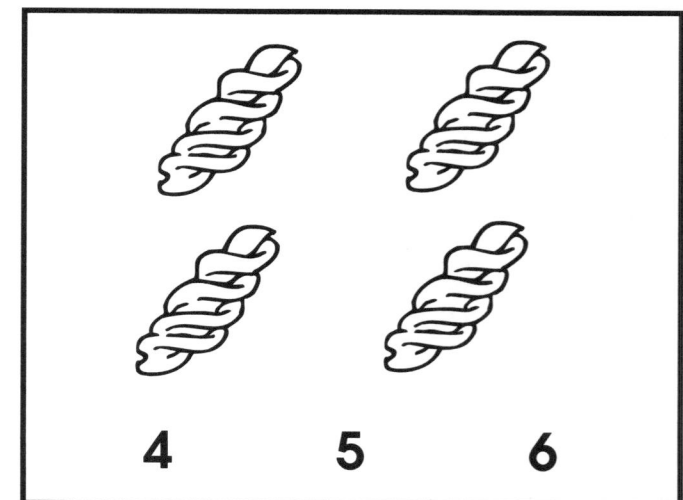

Pasta Dominoes

Use with "Pasta Dominoes" on page 12.

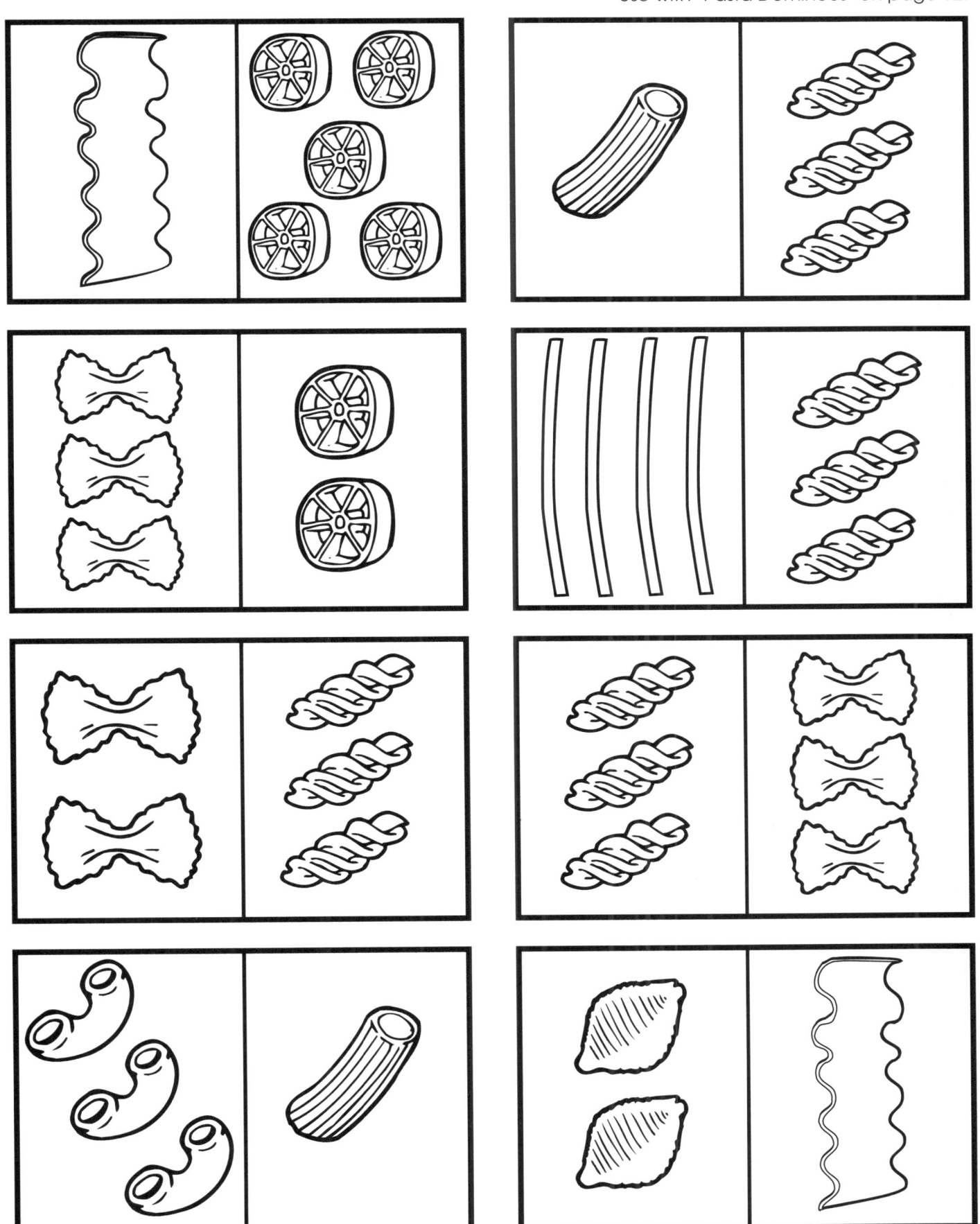

Pasta Dominoes
Use with "Pasta Dominoes" on page 12.

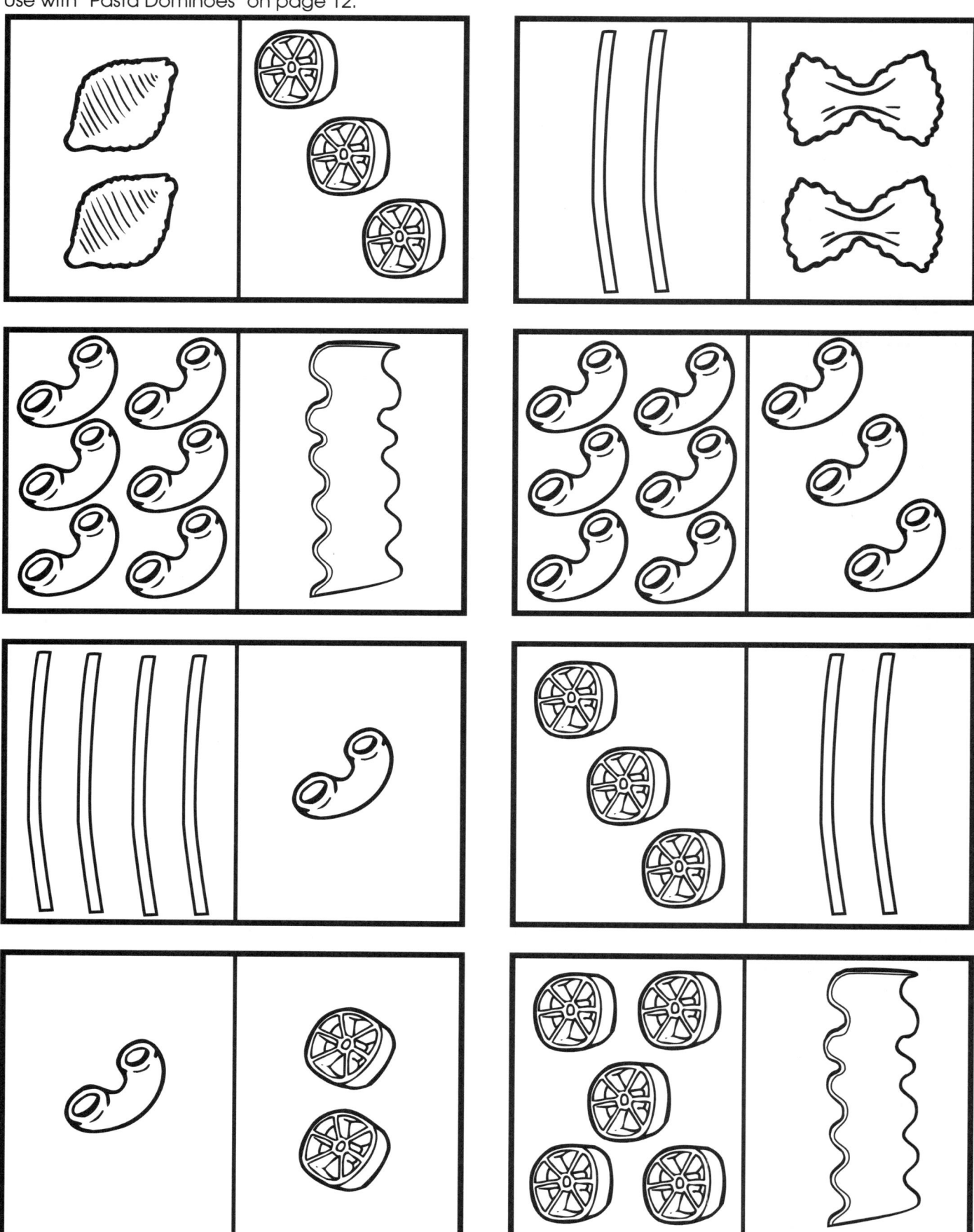

18 ©1999 The Education Center, Inc. • *October Monthly Reproducibles* • Kindergarten • TEC959

Get Poppin'!

Sizzle, sizzle, pop, pop! The popcorn's ready, so crunch and munch your way through October—National Popcorn Poppin' Month!

In The Popper
Promote phonemic awareness with this activity that reinforces the -op rime. Make a transparency from page 20. With the transparency on your overhead projector, read aloud one of the words to your class. Ask a student volunteer to tell you whether the word has the same ending as the word *pop*. If it does, have him come up and use a Vis-à-Vis® overhead projection pen to draw a fluffy popcorn shape around the word. If the word doesn't have the -op ending, have him draw a small oval around it, designating it as an unpopped kernel. Keep going until you've drawn a shape around each word in the popper.

A Popcorn String
Help youngsters practice spelling their names with these popcorn-string necklaces. To prepare, duplicate a class supply of page 21; then cut a class supply of 30-inch yarn lengths. If desired, give each child a name card to assist her with this activity.

To make a necklace, a child cuts out the number of rectangles equal to the number of letters in her name. Then she writes one letter from her name in each of the popcorn pieces on her cutouts. To assemble her necklace, she folds the rectangles over the length of yarn so that all the popcorn pieces are facing the same way and the letters of her name are in order. She glues each folded rectangle shut, then ties the yarn ends together to make a necklace (with help if necessary). These necklaces are sure to be "pop-ular" fashion items!

Weighty Matters
Which weighs more—popcorn or paper clips? Find out with this measurement activity. Duplicate page 22 for each child. Gather a supply of popcorn kernels and the other items shown on the reproducible. Place the items, the copies of page 22, and a balance scale at your math center. Have each child who visits the center weigh the pictured items, observe the result on the scale, and then shade in the box showing the heavier item. If he finds two items equal in weight, instruct him to shade both boxes in that pair. What a perfect balance of learning and fun!

Pop! Pop! Pop!
Which Words End In -op?

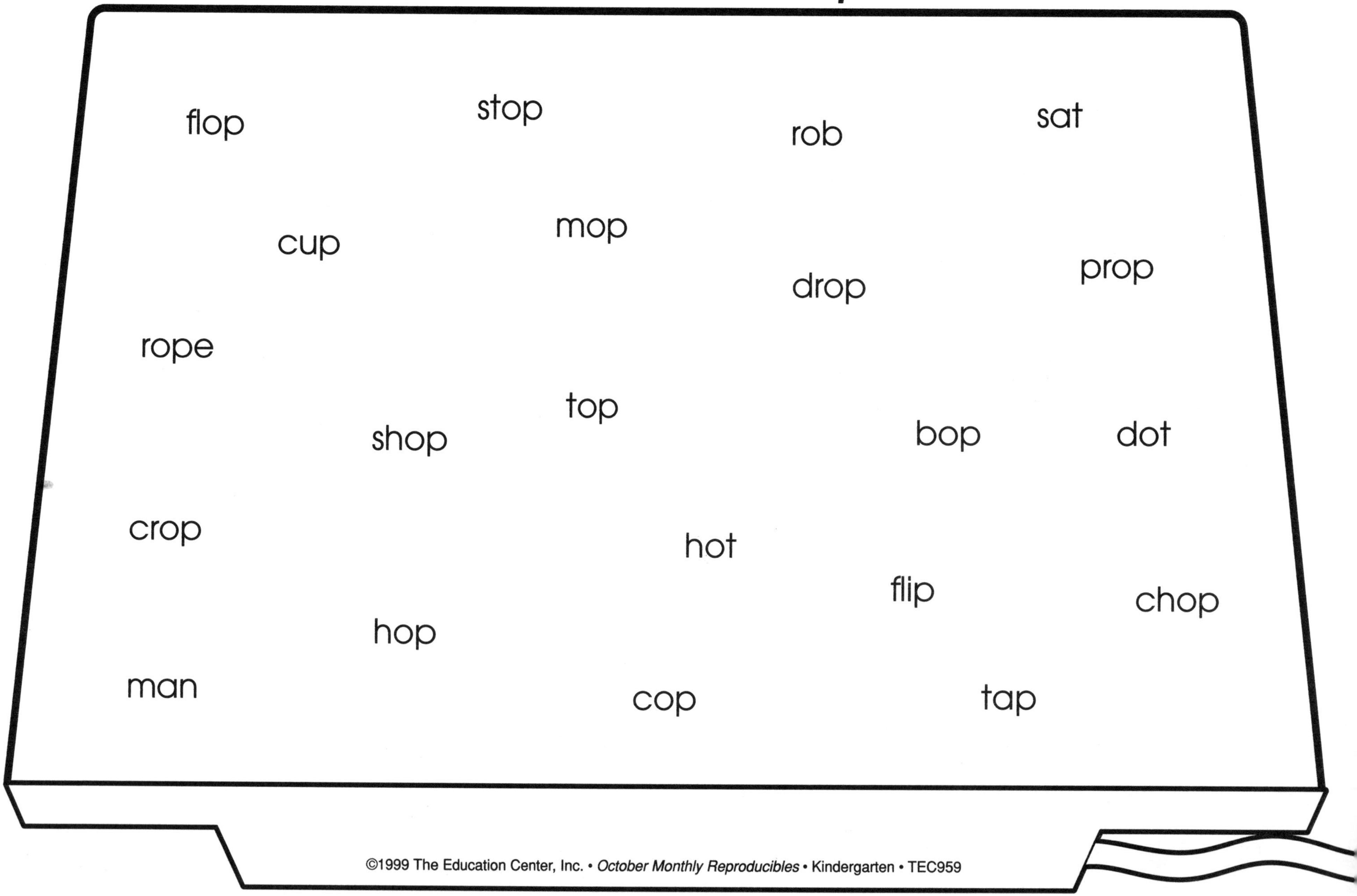

flop, cup, stop, mop, sat, rob, prop, drop, rope, shop, top, hot, bop, dot, crop, hop, cop, flip, chop, man, tap

©1999 The Education Center, Inc. • *October Monthly Reproducibles* • Kindergarten • TEC959

Necklace Patterns
Use with "A Popcorn String" on page 19.

Kernel Comparisons

Weigh each pair.
Shade the box that shows which is heavier.

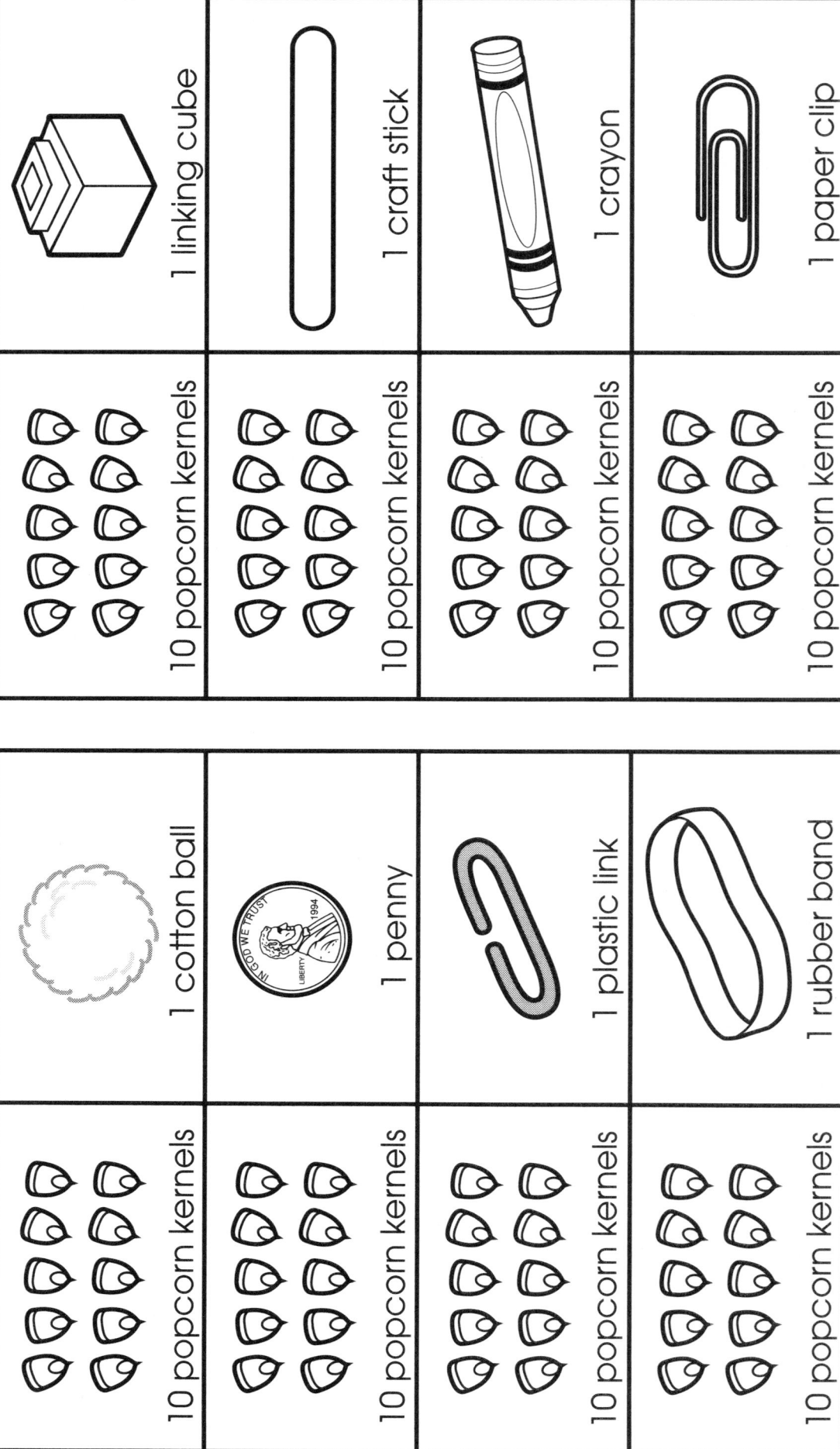

Fire Prevention Week

Sound the alarm—it's time for Fire Prevention Week! Use these ideas to spark some learning fun.

Deck The Hose With Safety Symbols

Use this idea to review items associated with Fire Prevention Week. Duplicate a copy of page 24; then discuss how each item relates to Fire Prevention Week. Next invite youngsters to make these fire-hose mobiles. For each child, duplicate page 24 onto white construction paper. Duplicate page 25 onto red construction paper; then laminate the page. To make a mobile, color the patterns, then cut them out. Be sure to follow the bold line along the outside and inside of the spiral. Glue the nozzle to the end of the hose. Punch small holes as indicated in the hose and at the top of each remaining cutout. Use a ten-inch length of heavy thread to tie each cutout to the hose. (Or do not punch holes and instead tape the cutouts to the thread and the thread to the hose.) To complete the mobile, tie a knot in one end of a ten-inch length of yarn. Thread the yarn through the hole at the top of the mobile; then tie the yarn into a loop for hanging.

Match Making

This fire-safety project is a clever way to remind students not to play with matches. For each child, duplicate page 26 onto white construction paper. To make a matchbook, color the matches; then cut out the matches and the poem. (For a realistic effect, paint the tips of the matches with red paint to which a small amount of sand has been added.) Fold up a 2 1/2" flap at the bottom of a 6" x 18" piece of construction paper. Glue a 1" x 6" strip of black construction paper to the front of this flap, and glue the matches behind the flap to complete the sentence "Do not play with matches!" Glue the flap over the matches, leaving the top edge of the flap loose. To complete the project, fold down the remainder of the construction paper so that it covers the matches and the end is tucked into the flap. Personalize the poem cutout, and then glue it to the front of the matchbook.

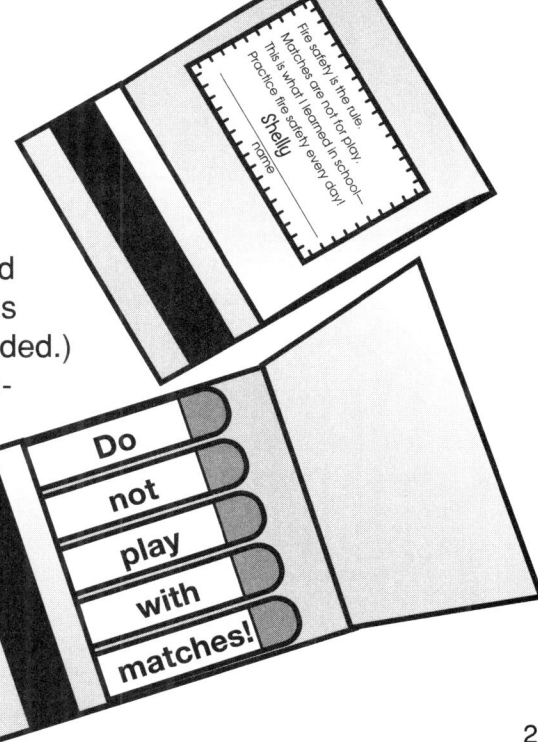

Mobile Patterns
Use with "Deck The Hose With Safety Symbols" on page 23.

Mobile Patterns
Use with "Deck The Hose With Safety Symbols" on page 23.

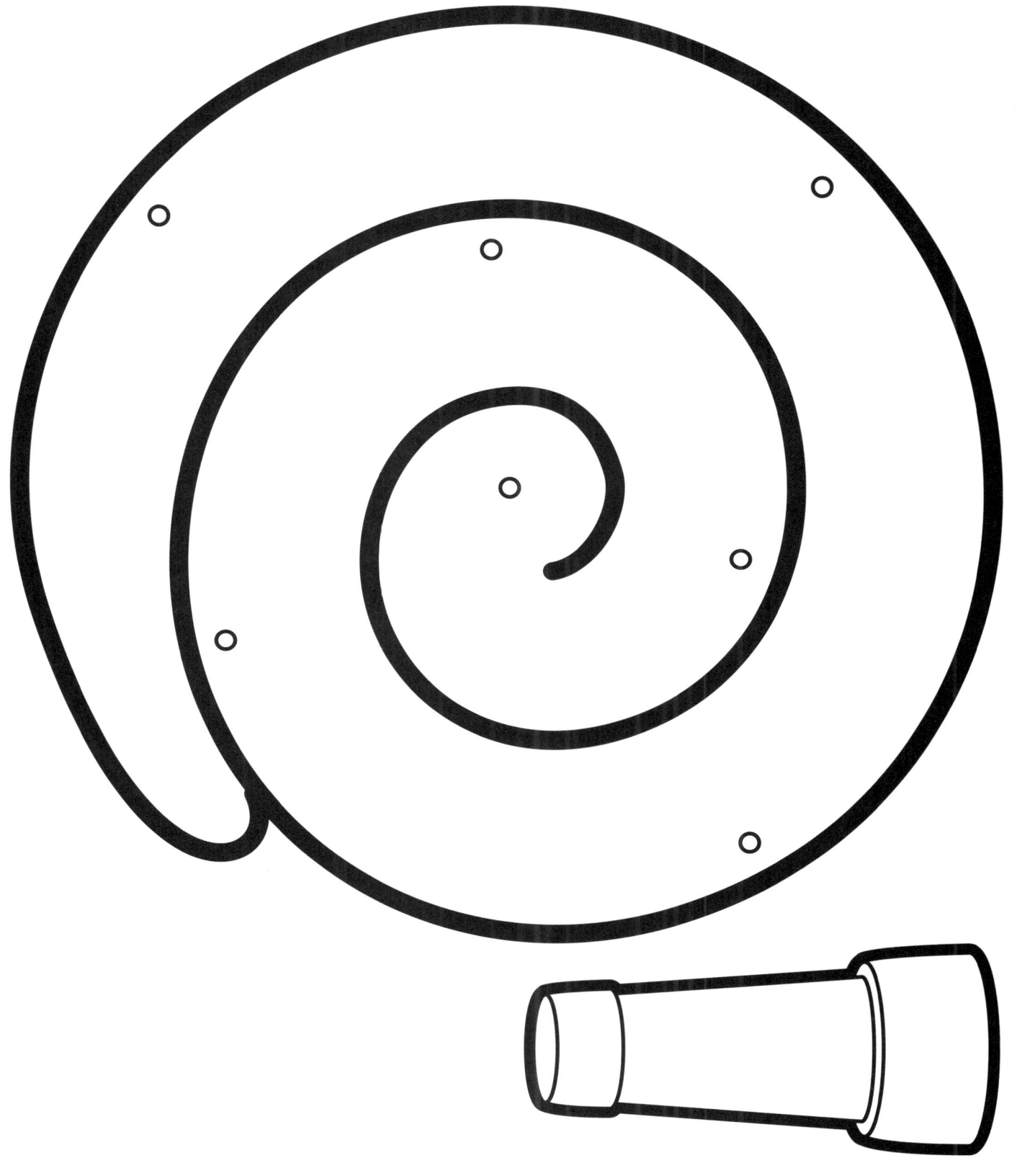

Matchbook Patterns
Use with "Match Making" on page 23.

Do

not

play

with

matches!

Fire safety is the rule.
Matches are not for play.
This is what I learned in school—
Practice fire safety every day!

_____
name

©1999 The Education Center, Inc. • *October Monthly Reproducibles* • Kindergarten • TEC959

All In The Family

To each of us, a family is something—and someone—different. Use these activities and reproducibles to help your students explore the meaning of family.

A Family Fill-In
Here's a fun way to have youngsters describe their families. Duplicate a copy of page 28 for each child. Give the following oral directions for each child to follow:

- Think about how many grown-ups live in your home. If there is only one, color the house green. If there is more than one, color the house yellow.
- Draw a cloud in the sky for each brother you have. If you don't have any brothers, don't draw any clouds.
- Draw a flower next to the house for each sister you have. If you don't have any sisters, don't draw any flowers.
- Color the tree green with a brown trunk. If you have a grandmother or grandfather living with you, add apples to the tree.
- Think about your pets. If you don't have a pet, color the car blue. If you have *one* pet, color it red. If you have *more than one* pet, color it purple.

Invite students to take turns sharing their finished pictures. They'll enjoy discovering the differences and similarities between their families.

Where Do You Fit In?
How can you tell the difference between children who are the oldest, the youngest, the middle, or the only children in their families? Ask them! Use the reproducible on page 29 to create a graph illustrating how your students break down by birth order. Duplicate the page onto tagboard; then cut out the house shapes. Attach the house shapes as column headers on a sheet of chart paper or on your chalkboard. Talk about each illustration. Then have each child mount his photo or name card in the appropriate column. Use the graph to spark discussions about the benefits and challenges children might encounter in each birth-order position.

Hugs All Around!
Your study of families is sure to lead to one conclusion: families are all about love! Invite your students to create these bear hugs as expressions of love for their families. To prepare, ask each child to bring in a 3" x 5" or 4" x 6" photo of her family. Duplicate the patterns on page 30 onto brown construction paper for each child. Help each child cut out all her patterns, including the dotted-line heart shape. Have her tape her photo to the back of the bear body pattern so that her family shows in the heart-shaped opening. Trim the edges of the photo as necessary. Staple the two arms in place as shown. Send home the finished projects, encouraging youngsters to fold open the arms to show off their "bear-y" special families!

Name _____

All In The Family
Listening skills

Bear-Hug Patterns
Use with "Hugs All Around!" on page 27.

'Tis The Season For... LEAVES!

Orange, yellow, red, and brown—autumn leaves are all around! Investigate these natural beauties with the help of these fun reproducibles.

Looking For Leaves

Are you planning to take your youngsters on a hunt for autumn leaves? Add to the fun—and learning—with these cute leaf-collection bags. Duplicate the patterns on page 33 for each child. Invite each youngster to color the squirrel and leaves and personalize the bag label. If desired, provide wiggle eyes for each child to glue onto the squirrel's face. Have each youngster cut out his bag label, then glue it to one side of a small paper lunch bag. (Set the record sheet aside for later.) Have your kindergartners take their bags along when you hunt for autumn leaves.

When you return to the classroom, invite each child to empty his bag and sort his leaves by color. Guide the students to color the leaves on their record sheets appropriately. Then help each child use tally marks or numerals to fill in the blank beside each leaf to reflect his collection. Have each child glue his completed record sheet to the plain side of his leaf-collection bag before returning the leaves to the bag and taking his collection home to recount with Mom or Dad.

Bag It!

Couple math and fine-motor skills with the reproducible on page 34. Duplicate the page for each child. Invite students to use one of the following methods to make a corresponding set of leaves within each bag outline:

— Using a stamp pad in an autumn color, make the correct number of fingerprint leaves inside each bag outline.

— Peel and stick the correct number of leaf stickers within each bag outline.

— Using a rubber stamp with a leaf design and a stamp pad in an autumn color, stamp the correct number of leaves within each outline.

— Glue the correct number of construction paper–scrap leaves (in autumn colors) within each outline.

Jump In The Pile

Here's a fun-for-fall version of the classic game "Go Fish." To prepare, duplicate two copies of the leaf cards on page 35 onto tagboard. Color the cards so that you have seven sets, each with four matching leaves. Laminate the cards for durability.

To play, each child in a pair takes five cards from the mixed-up deck. The remaining cards are placed facedown in a pile. Each child first pulls out all the matching pairs from his hand, laying them on the table. Then one player begins by showing his partner one card from his hand. If his partner has a match, she must give up the card. If his partner does not have a match when shown a card, she says, "Jump in the pile!" The child who requested a card may then draw from the facedown pile, attempting to find a match. The object of the game is to get the most pairs before the cards run out. Vary the game by having players attempt to get all four cards before laying down a matched set.

Leafy Literature

Why Do Leaves Change Color?
Written by Betsy Maestro
Published by HarperCollins Children's Books

Red Leaf, Yellow Leaf
Written by Lois Ehlert
Published by Harcourt Brace Jovanovich

Fall Is Not Easy
Written by Marty Kelley
Published by Zino Press

Fall Colors

Review autumn color words—and their beginning letters—with the reproducible on page 36.

Leafy Options

Use the leaf cards created for "Jump In The Pile" to play a game of Leaf Concentration. Simply place all the cards facedown in a grid formation. Invite pairs or small groups to play, taking turns flipping over two cards at a time, attempting to find matches. Add a real memory challenge by asking players to turn over four cards at a time and locate the four matching cards in each set!

As an alternative, place the leaf cards in your math center and encourage youngsters to use them for patterning practice. To follow up, duplicate two copies of page 35 for each child. Invite each student to choose two types of leaves to color and cut out. Have her make a pattern on a strip of construction paper, then glue it in place. Use the finished strips as a bulletin-board border or as frames for student artwork. How lovely and leafy!

Bag Label And Record Sheet

Use with "Looking For Leaves" on page 31.

I'm Looking For Leaves!

I looked for leaves.
I found: 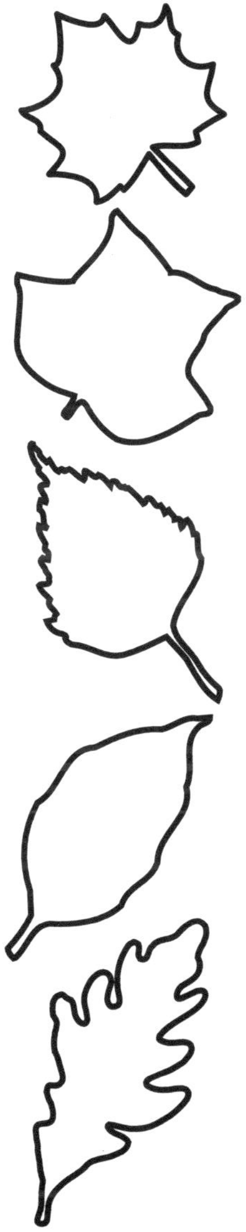
_____ **red** leaves
_____ **yellow** leaves
_____ **brown** leaves
_____ **orange** leaves
_____ leaves with **lots of colors**

Name _____

'Tis The Season For...Leaves!
Creating sets

In The Bag

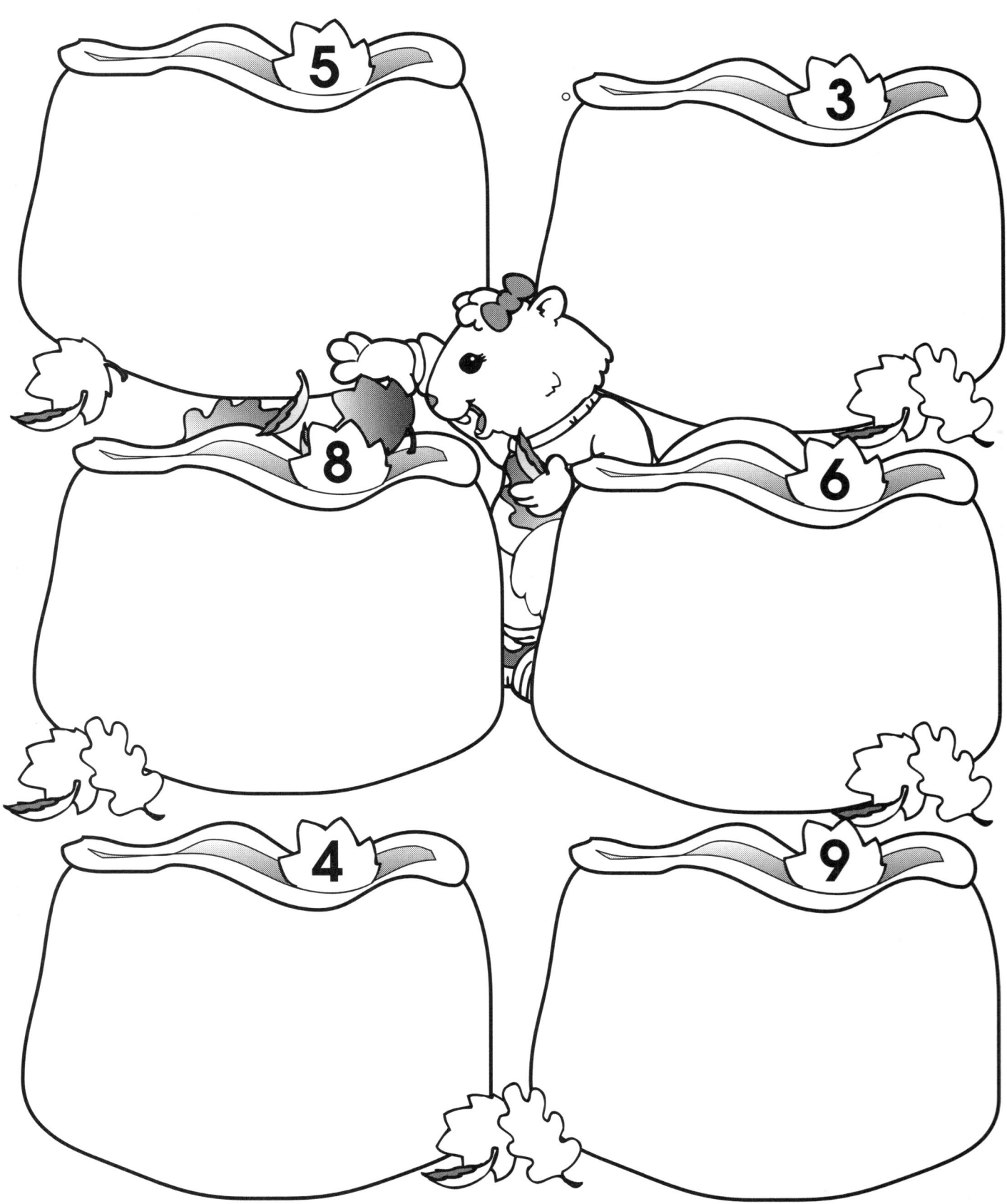

Leaf Cards

Use with "Jump In The Pile" and "Leafy Options" on page 32.

Fabulous Foliage

🖍 Color by the code.

Y = yellow
R = red
B = brown
O = orange

IN THE PUMPKIN PATCH

Harvest skills in language, math, and critical thinking when you take a trip to the pumpkin patch. Let's go!

Pumpkins Of All Sizes

Pumpkins are well suited to sorting by size. If you've got a class collection of pumpkins from parent donations or from a trip to a real pumpkin patch, invite youngsters to sort the pumpkins into three categories—small, medium, and large. Or bring in just one pumpkin of each size for students to compare. Then have each student complete a copy of page 38. Ask each child to color the pumpkins at the bottom of her sheet, then cut them apart and glue them in the correct rows of the pumpkin patch.

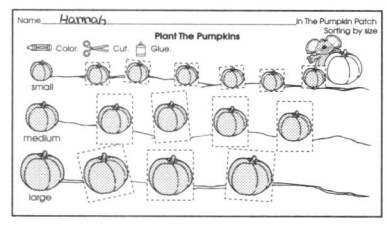

The Perfect Pumpkin

This critical-thinking activity will have your students poring over the patch to find the perfect pumpkin—the one revealed by the clues below! Duplicate a class supply of page 39; then distribute a copy to each child. Read aloud one clue at a time, and have students cross out any pumpkin that doesn't fit the description. After the last pumpkins are eliminated, only one will be left. Invite each student to draw and color a blue ribbon on this perfect pumpkin. Listening and thinking—those make *everyone* a winner!

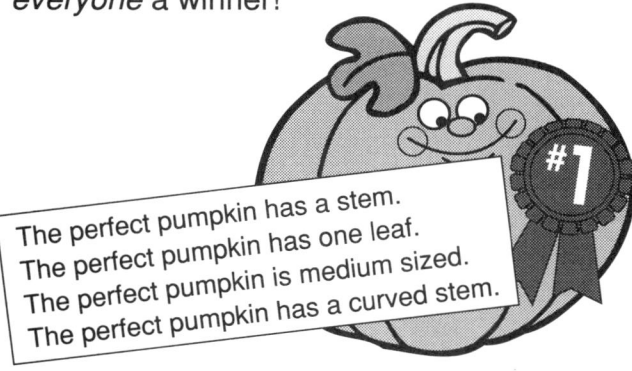

The perfect pumpkin has a stem.
The perfect pumpkin has one leaf.
The perfect pumpkin is medium sized.
The perfect pumpkin has a curved stem.

P Is For Pumpkin Patch

This trip through the pumpkin patch will reinforce the sound of the letter *p*. To prepare, duplicate the gameboard and playing cards on pages 40–42 onto tagboard. Color and cut out the two gameboard pieces; then tape them together and laminate the finished board for durability. If desired, also laminate the cards before cutting them apart. Provide each player with a candy pumpkin to use as a game marker. Place the cards in a pile facedown where indicated.

To play, each player in a small group takes a turn drawing a card. She identifies the picture on the card. If the item begins with a *p* sound, she moves her game marker forward one space and follows any directions written on the gameboard. If the pictured item does not begin with a *p* sound, she does not move her marker. (If necessary, reshuffle the discard pile and reuse the cards.) As each player makes her way out of the patch, invite her to eat her candy-pumpkin game marker. Hey, let's play that pumpkin-patch game again!

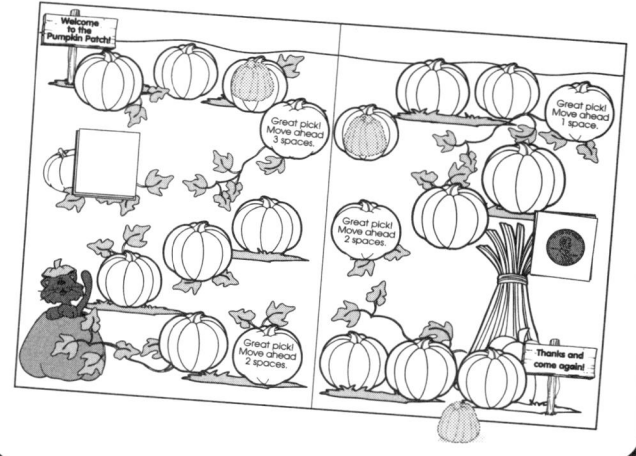

Name _____

Plant The Pumpkins

🖍 Color. ✂ Cut. 🧴 Glue.

small

medium

large

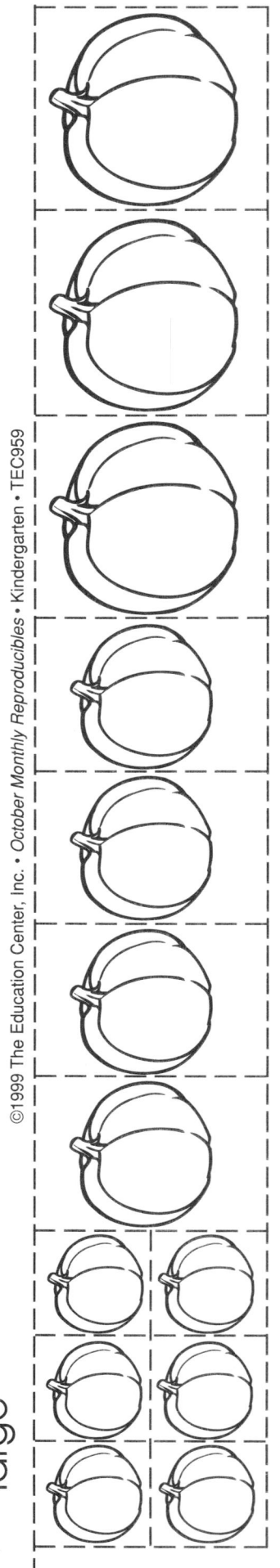

In The Pumpkin Patch
Sorting by size

©1999 The Education Center, Inc. • *October Monthly Reproducibles* • Kindergarten • TEC959

Name _____

In The Pumpkin Patch
Critical thinking

The Perfect Pumpkin

Listen to the clues.

🖍 Draw Xs.   🖍 Draw a blue ribbon.

©1999 The Education Center, Inc. • *October Monthly Reproducibles* • Kindergarten • TEC959

Gameboard
Use with "*P* Is For Pumpkin Patch" on page 37.

Gameboard

Use with "*P* Is For Pumpkin Patch" on page 37.

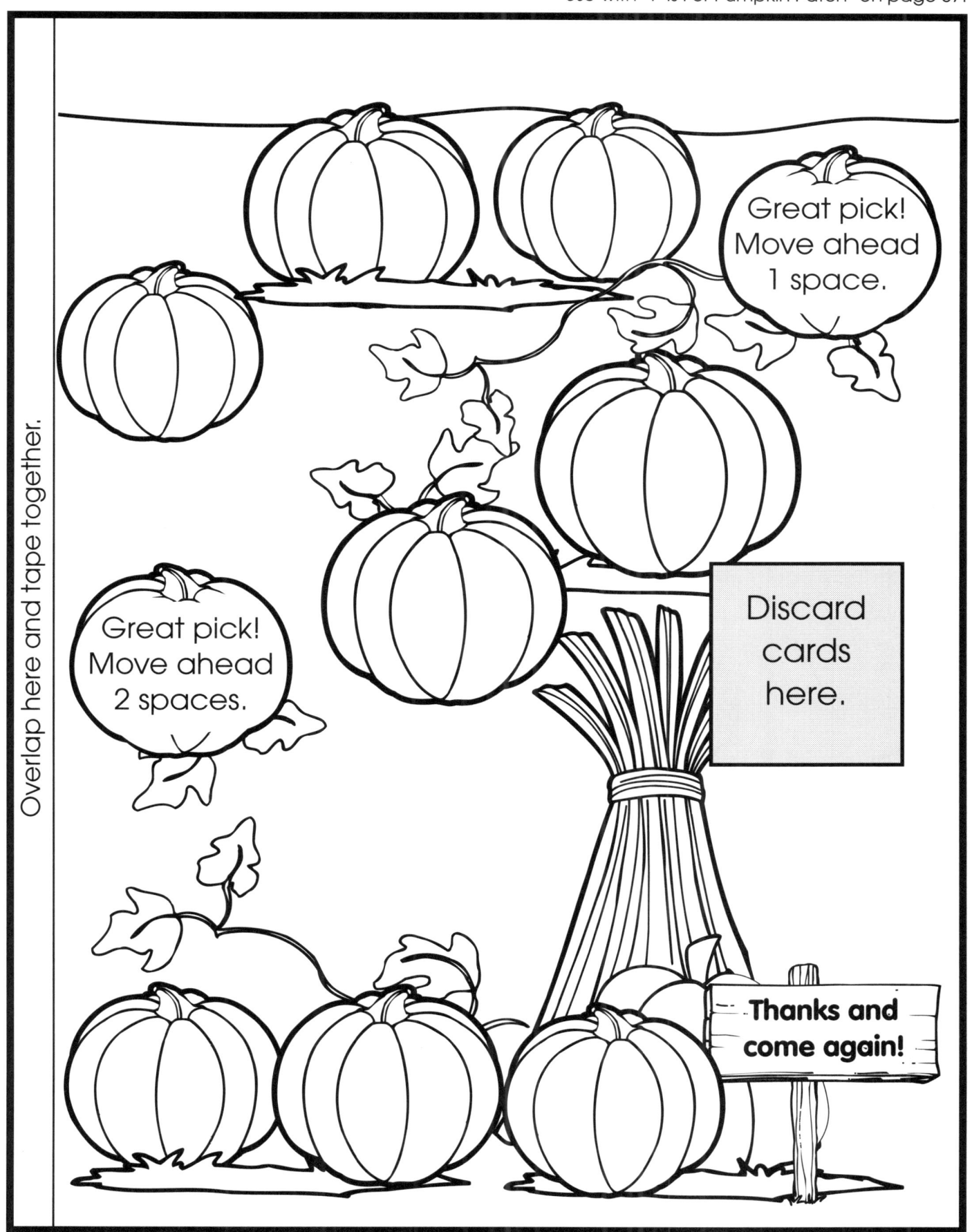

Cards
Use with *"P Is For Pumpkin Patch"* on page 37.

Spiffy Spiders

Whether you love 'em or loathe 'em, spiders are very interesting to study. Try these "spider-riffic" learning activities to help youngsters learn more about these eight-legged wonders.

Colorful Creepy-Crawly
These cute crawlers will help little ones with color-word recognition. Duplicate a class supply of page 45; then encourage each student to color his sheet according to the key. Display the completed sheets with the caption "Colorful Creepy-Crawlies Are Cool!"

Spider-Search Graph
Practice graphing skills with the spidery reproducible on page 46. Direct each of your little spider searchers to look carefully at each spider on her paper. Have each child color the happy spiders red and the sad spiders blue. Then have each child graph the spiders of each color. Spiders, spiders everywhere!

Five Little Spiders
Teach this spunky spider fingerplay to your students. If desired, provide plastic spider rings and invite children to take turns wearing the rings as they act out the verse.

Five little spiders crawling all around,
The first one said, "See the bug I found?"
The second one said, "My web is neat."
The third one said, "I have eight feet."
The fourth one said, "We're all so small."
The fifth one said, "Time for autumn leaves to fall!"
Then whoosh went the wind and out went the light
And the five little spiders crawled out of sight!

Eight Guesses To Go

Play this flannelboard game with students to develop their numeral-recognition skills. Make one copy of the spider face and four copies of the spider legs on page 47 on construction paper; then cut out all the pieces and laminate them for durability. Cut six index cards in half. Label each half with a different numeral from 1 to 12. Attach the hook side of a strip of self-adhesive Velcro® to the back of each numeral card and spider piece.

To play the game, attach the spider body to your flannelboard. Tell students you are thinking of a number from 1 to 12. Invite students to take up to eight chances to guess your secret numeral. Attach one spider leg for each incorrect numeral guessed. Attach each guessed numeral to the flannelboard so it won't be guessed again. Challenge your youngsters to guess the secret numeral before all eight legs are attached to the spider. Go on—take a guess!

"Spider-riffic" Cover-Ups

Need a treat for your little tricksters? Try this crafty project that's sure to please a roomful of spider fans. In advance, purchase a class supply of wrapped, flat lollipops. Duplicate a copy of the spider patterns on page 48 onto white construction paper for each child. To make one cover-up, color the spider pieces black; then cut them out. Fold the body pattern as indicated; then glue the legs on the inside of the body as shown. Glue the side edges of the body piece together, leaving the bottom open for the lollipop. When the glue is dry, fold each leg downward for a three-dimensional effect. Slip a wrapped lollipop into each cover-up, and send home these spidery sweet treats!

Spider Send-Off

Wrap up your spider study with these student awards. Duplicate a copy of the award pattern on page 48 for each child. Fill in the child's name and the date; then sign the award. Youngsters will be proud to receive these arachnid awards!

Name _____

Spiffy Spiders
Color words

Colorful Creepy-Crawly

Color:
- bow = green
- hat = red
- shoe = blue
- face = yellow

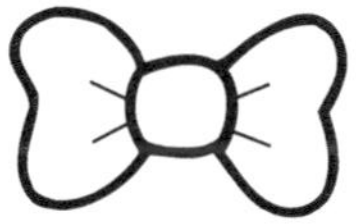

©1999 The Education Center, Inc. • *October Monthly Reproducibles* • Kindergarten • TEC959

45

Name _____

Spiffy Spiders
Graphing

Spider Search

Color the happy spiders red.
Color the sad spiders blue.
Graph.

How many spiders are happy?

How many spiders are sad?

46 ©1999 The Education Center, Inc. • *October Monthly Reproducibles* • Kindergarten • TEC959

Spider Patterns
Use with "Eight Guesses To Go" on page 44.

Patterns
Use with " 'Spider-riffic' Cover-Ups" on page 44.

Award
Use with "Spider Send-Off" on page 44.

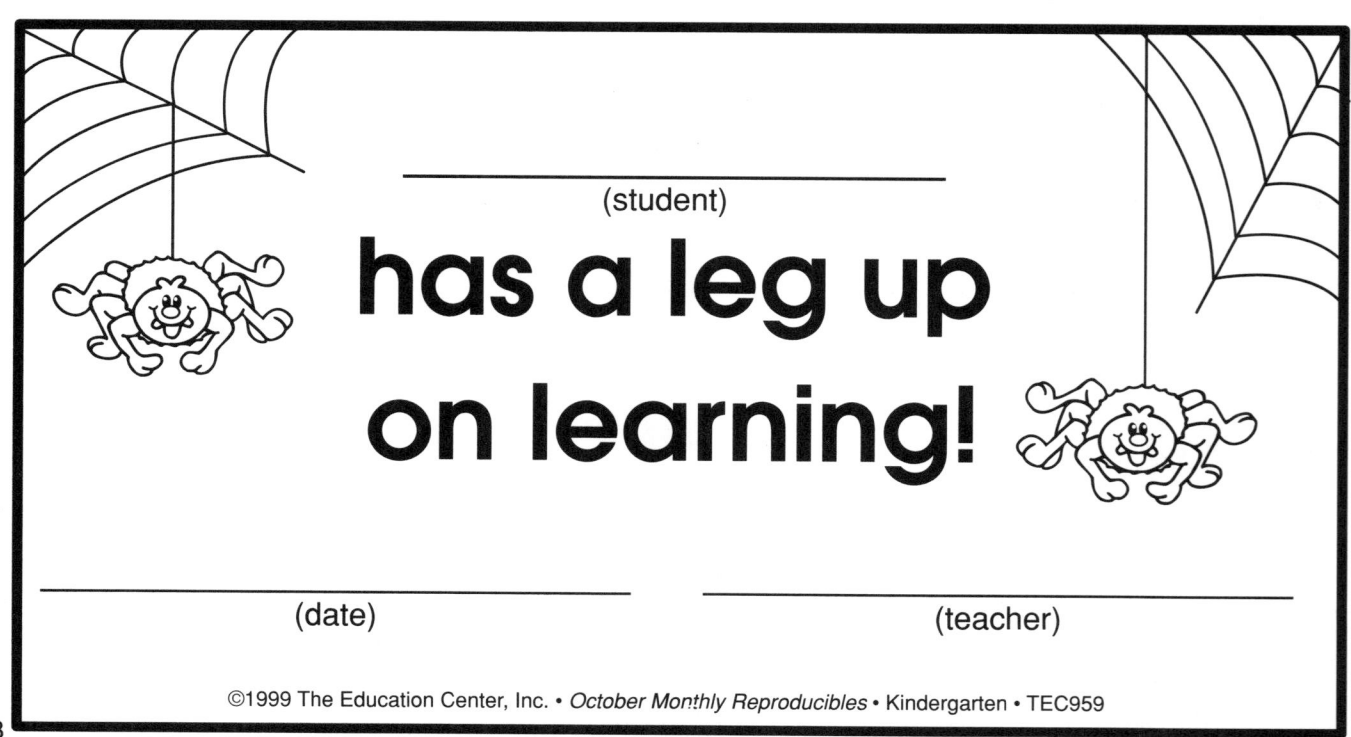

_____
(student)

has a leg up on learning!

_____   _____
(date)   (teacher)

With its costumes, candy, and creepy critters, Halloween is such a colorful holiday. So concentrate on colors and color words with this reproducible booklet your boys and "ghouls" will love!

Halloween Colors Booklet

Invite youngsters to illustrate the reproducible booklet on pages 50–56 in seasonal shades. To prepare, duplicate the booklet cover and pages onto white construction paper for each child. To make a booklet, a child cuts out her cover and pages, then follows the directions below to complete each page.

If you choose to have students complete the booklet over several work sessions, you may want to use the booklet cover as a management tool. As a child completes a page, have her use the corresponding color to fill in one letter in the word *colors* on her booklet cover. Once all the pages are complete, each color from the booklet will be represented on her booklet cover. Help each child sequence her pages; then staple her booklet along the left side.

Cover: Color the crayon as desired. Cut it out; then glue it to the cover. Write your name on the line.

Page 1: Draw a black mouth on the pumpkin; then color the pumpkin orange. Color the eyes and nose black; then cut them out and glue them to the pumpkin to complete the face.

Page 2: Color the cat and the tail pattern black. Cut out the tail; then glue it in place. Glue two wiggle eyes on the cat's face.

Page 3: Color the moon and the mouth pattern yellow. Cut out the mouth; then glue it in place. Decorate the stars with gold glitter.

Page 4: Color the bat body and head pattern brown. Cut out the bat head; then glue it in place. Use a brown crayon to draw and color two bat wings.

Page 5: Color the two parts of the apple red with a brown stem. Cut out the pattern; then glue it in place. Decorate the candy coating on the apple with red glitter.

Page 6: Color the mask pattern green. Cut out the mask; then staple it in place as indicated. Fold the mask up and draw two eyes beneath the mask. Draw a nose and mouth to complete the face.

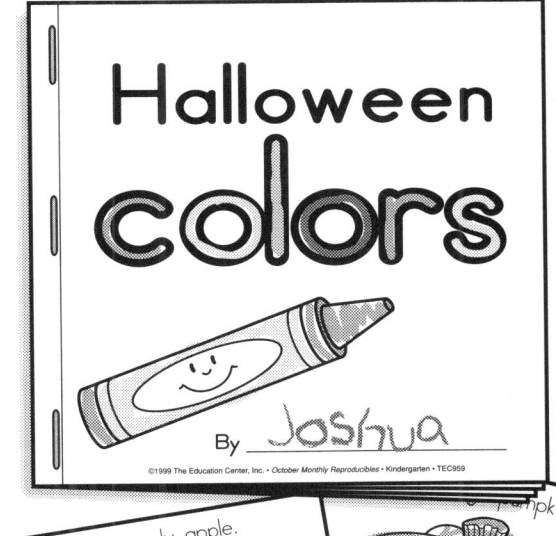

Booklet Cover
Use with "Halloween Colors Booklet" on page 49.

Halloween Colors

By _____

©1999 The Education Center, Inc. • *October Monthly Reproducibles* • Kindergarten • TEC959

Color.
Cut.
Glue.
Write your name.

Booklet Page 1
Use with "Halloween Colors Booklet" on page 49.

I see an orange pumpkin.

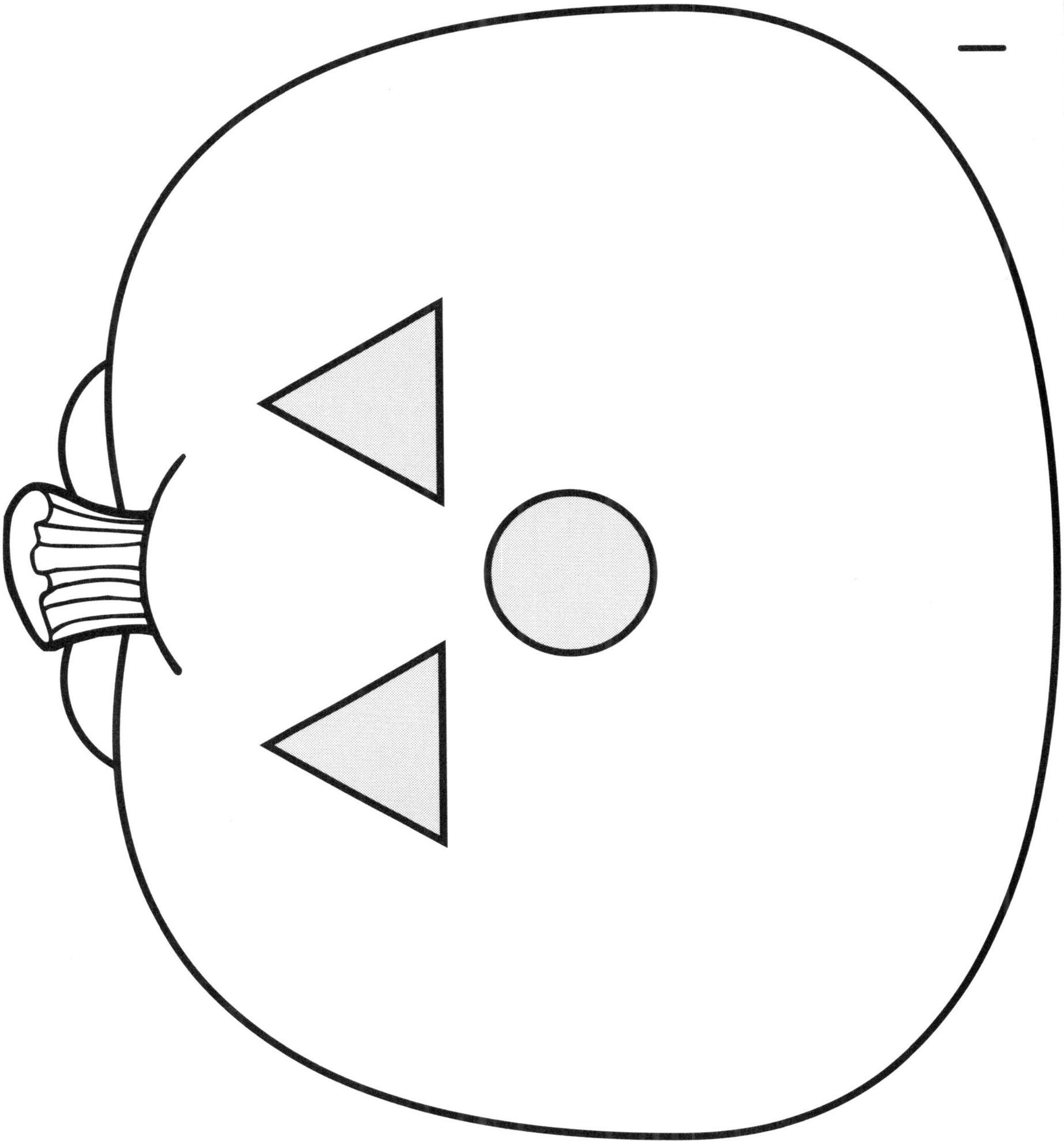

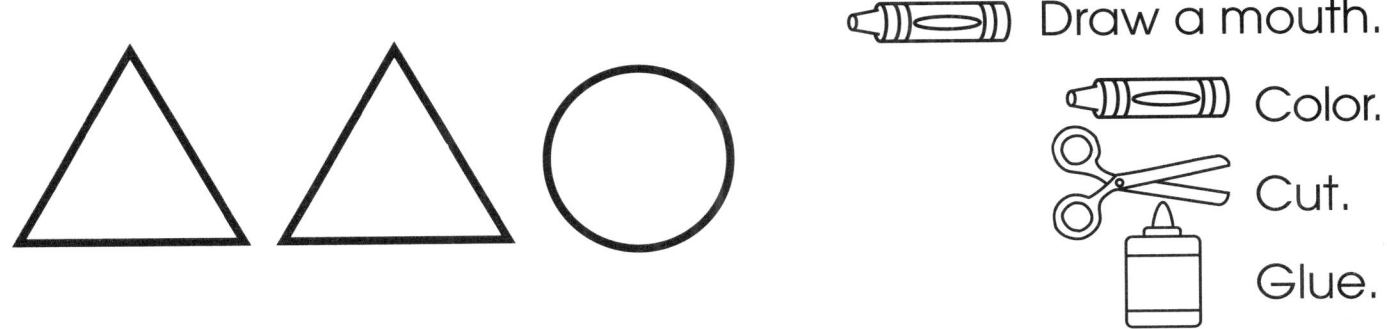

Draw a mouth.
Color.
Cut.
Glue.

Booklet Page 2
Use with "Halloween Colors Booklet" on page 49.

I see a black cat.

2

Color.
Cut.
Glue.

Add two eyes.

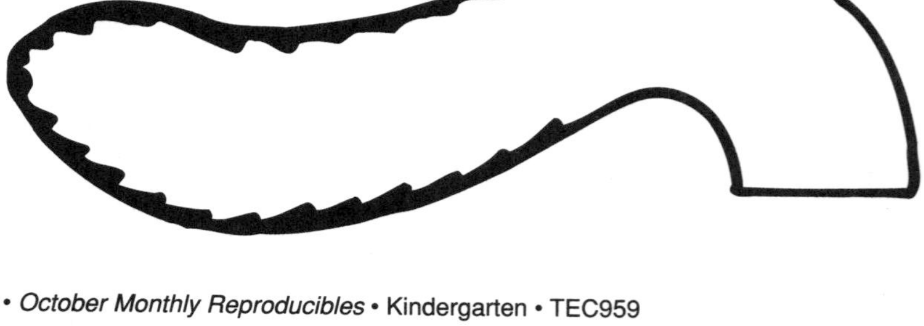

Booklet Page 3
Use with "Halloween Colors Booklet" on page 49.

I see a yellow moon.

Color.
Cut.
Glue.
Make glitter stars.

Booklet Page 4
Use with "Halloween Colors Booklet" on page 49.

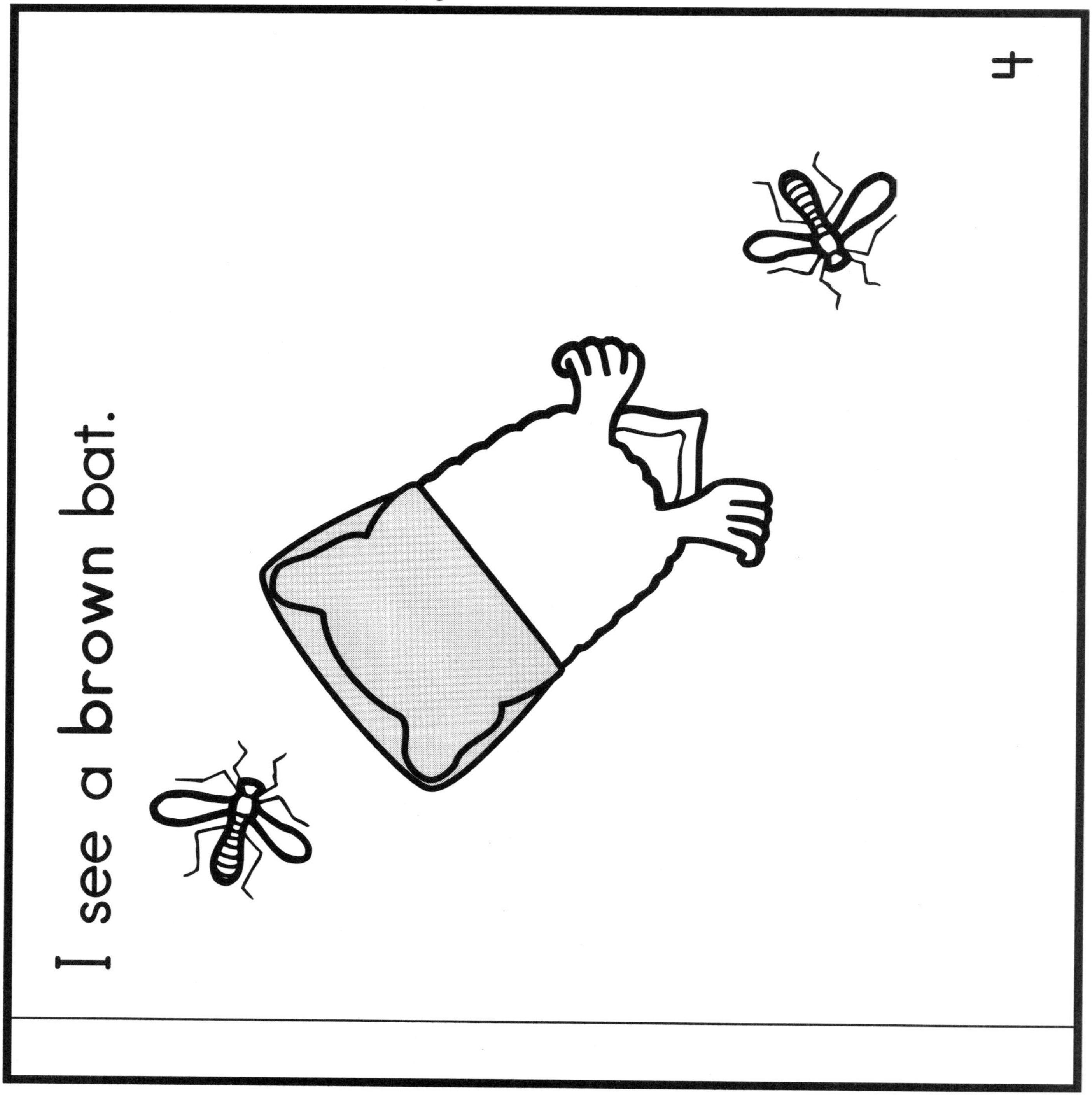

I see a brown bat.

Color.
Cut.
Glue.
Draw and color two wings.

Booklet Page 5
Use with "Halloween Colors Booklet" on page 49.

I see a red candy apple.

5

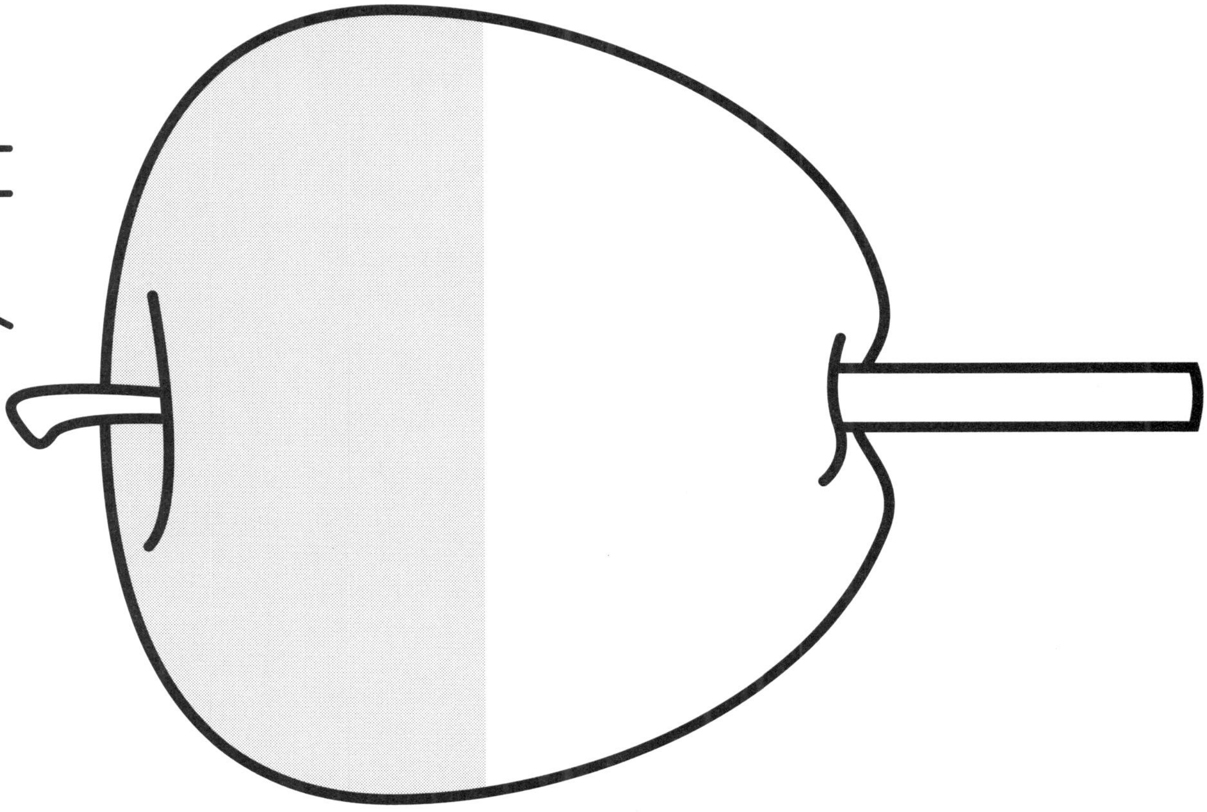

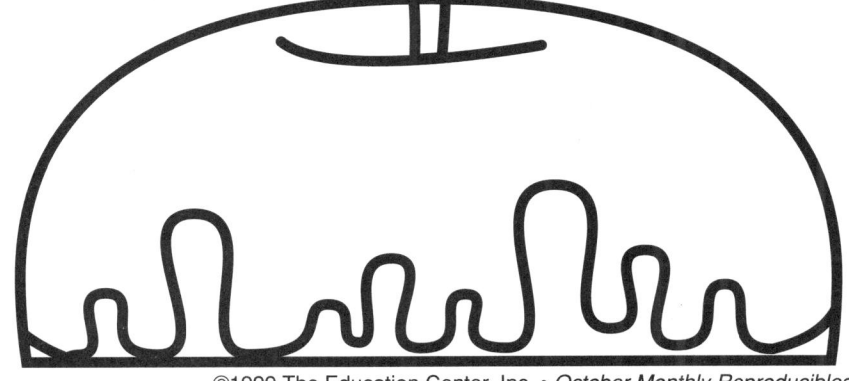

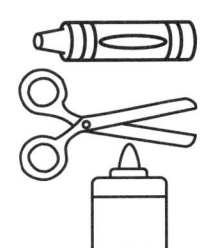

Color.

Cut.

Glue.

Add red glitter.

Booklet Page 6

Use with "Halloween Colors Booklet" on page 49.

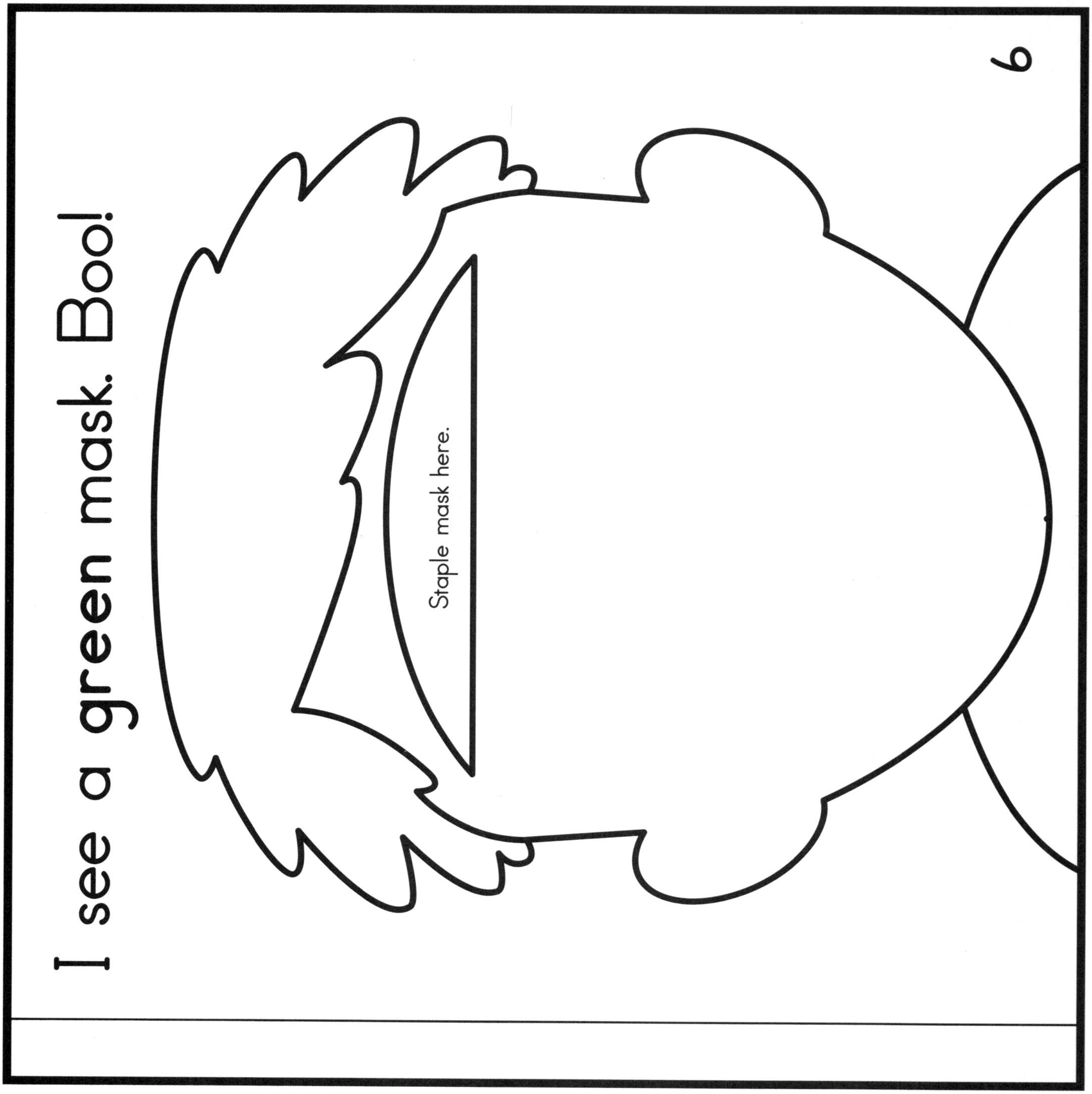

6
I see a green mask. Boo!
Staple mask here.

Color.

Cut.

Staple.

Draw a face.

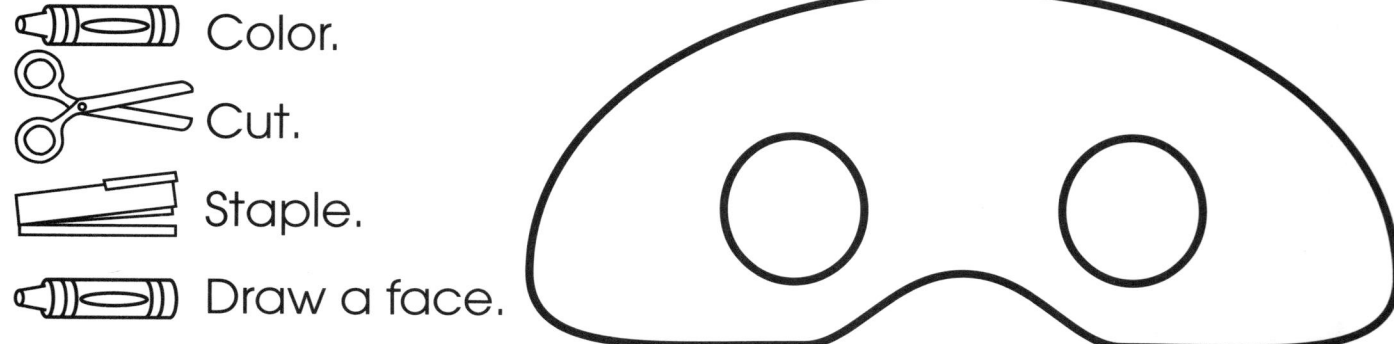

IT'S NIGHTTIME!

The sun has set, supper is finished, and you're getting sleepy. That's right—it's nighttime. Put on your fuzzy slippers and relax with this collection of nighttime activities and reproducibles. Nighty night!

The Difference Between Night And Day

This adorable doorknob hanger provides an interactive review of different activities and objects used at night and during the day. To make one, a child colors a copy of page 59. He cuts out the sun pocket, the moon pocket, and the doorknob hanger. He glues one pocket onto each side of the doorknob hanger, being careful to leave the top edge of each pocket loose. He then cuts apart the picture cards, sorts them, and puts them into the corresponding pockets. Invite each student to hang his doorknob hanger on a doorknob at home, flipping it to match the correct time of day.

My Bedtime Story

Little ones will love this bedtime story booklet they create themselves! To prepare, duplicate pages 60–63 on white construction paper for each child. Have each youngster cut apart her booklet pages. Invite each child to follow the directions below to complete her booklet:

Cover: Color the moon and stars with a gold or silver crayon. Write your name on the line.
Page 1: Add star stickers to the sky.
Page 2: Color the moon with a yellow highlighter.
Page 3: Color a craft stick and glue it over the toothbrush handle.
Page 4: Color the teddy bear and glue on two wiggle eyes.
Page 5: Draw yourself wearing the pajamas.
Page 6: Tape a short piece of string to the lampshade to resemble a pull chain.
Page 7: Glue a 2" x 3" fabric scrap over the child to resemble a blanket.

Once each child has completed all her pages, help her sequence them and staple the booklet along the left edge.

Nighty Night
Teach your little sleepyheads this fingerplay to soothe them to sleep!

1. I laughed and played throughout the day

2. And now there's one thing left to say:

3. "Please don't make the smallest peep;

4. I really need to get my sleep!"

MIDNIGHT MUNCHIE SNACK ATTACK

Snack Attack!
These cute containers hold just the right amount of treats to satisfy a nighttime munchie snack attack—or even a midday, let's-pretend-it's-nighttime snack attack! To prepare, duplicate a copy of page 64 for each child. To make a snack holder, cut off the recipe card and set it aside. Color the snack-holder pattern; then fold the flaps as indicated and glue them in place. Provide the ingredients shown on the recipe card, along with a small coffee scoop. Invite each child to follow the steps to whip up a tasty treat. Have each child take home her snack holder and recipe card to satisfy a *real* case of the midnight munchies!

What Do You Do At Night?
Everybody has a favorite evening pastime, whether it's unwinding in a bubble bath or curling up with a good book. Find out what your kindergartners enjoy with this graphing activity. Make a large graph labeled as shown; then provide each child with a star cutout on which to write her name and draw her face. After discussing evening activities with students, have each child choose her favorite to complete the graph.

Doorknob Hanger Pattern And Picture Cards
Use with "The Difference Between Night And Day" on page 57.

daytime

nighttime

Cut out.

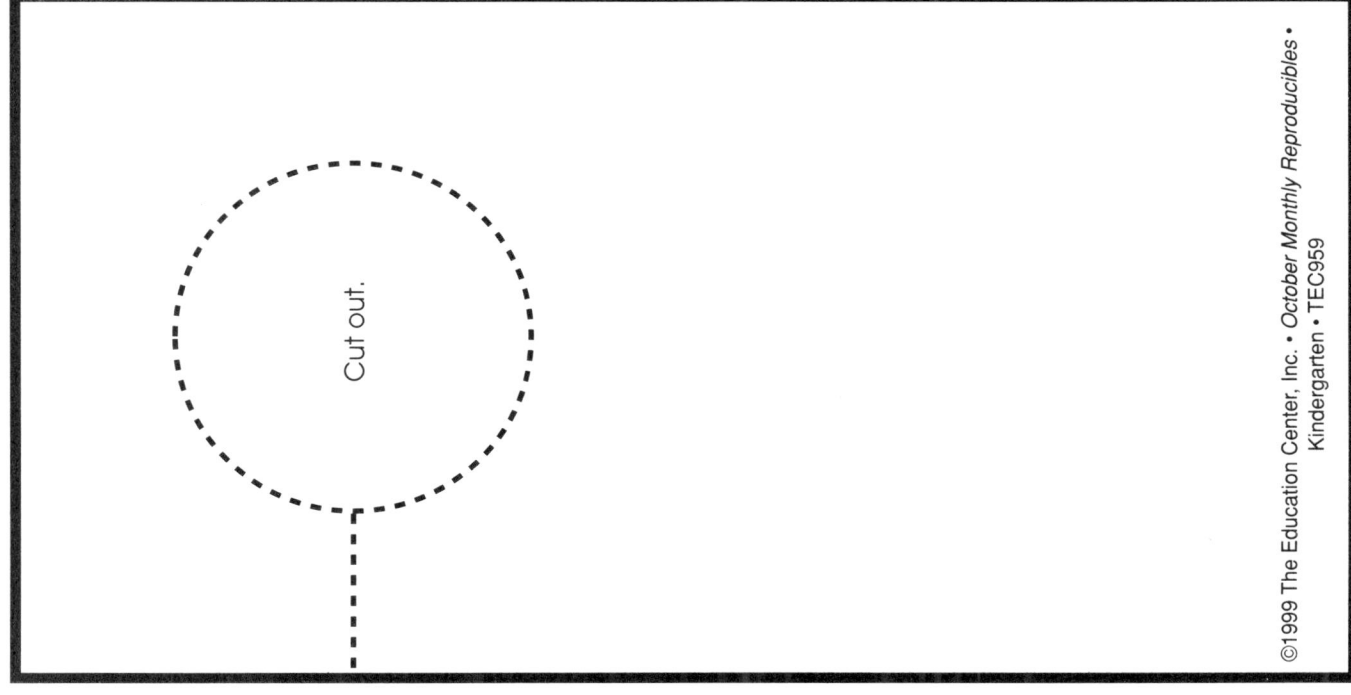

©1999 The Education Center, Inc. • *October Monthly Reproducibles* • Kindergarten • TEC959

Booklet Cover And Booklet Page 1
Use with "My Bedtime Story" on page 57.

Good Night, Sleep Tight!

Illustrated by:

_____

©1999 The Education Center, Inc. • *October Monthly Reproducibles* • Kindergarten • TEC959

When I look at the stars at night,

1

Booklet Pages 2 And 3
Use with "My Bedtime Story" on page 57.

I see the moon glow oh so bright.

2

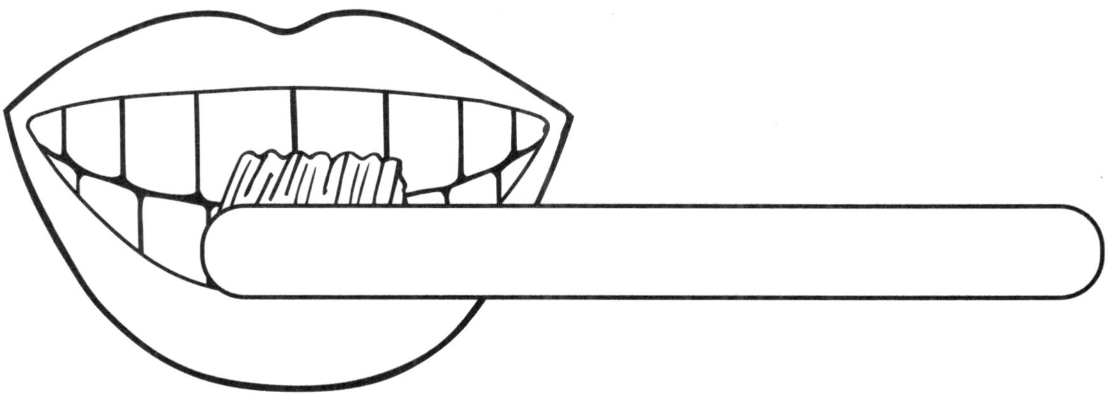

I brush my teeth to keep them white,

3

Booklet Pages 4 And 5
Use with "My Bedtime Story" on page 57.

Then grab my bear and hold him tight.

4

I put on pj's, oh what a sight!

5

Booklet Pages 6 And 7
Use with "My Bedtime Story" on page 57.

I turn off each and every light.

6

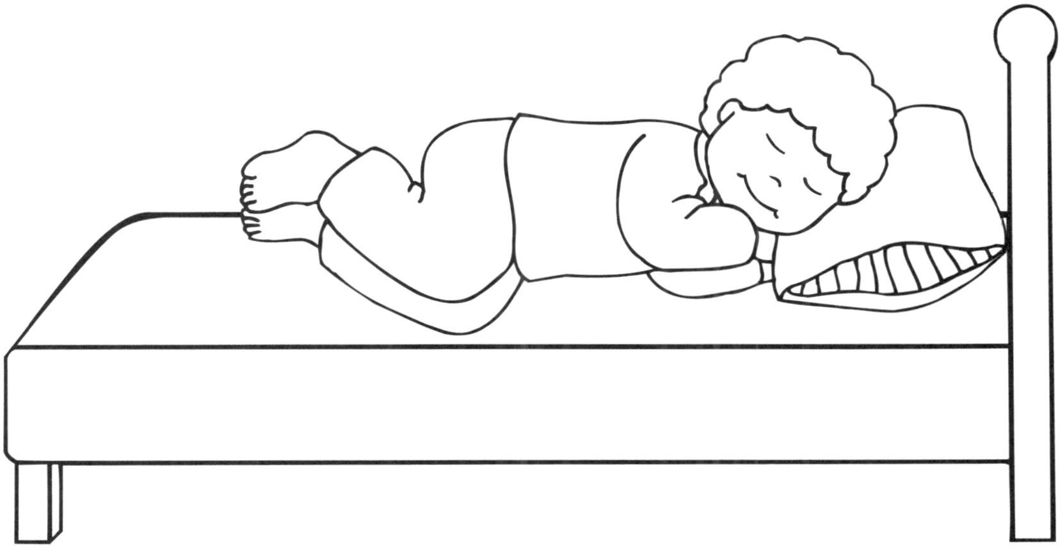

Then I climb into bed and say, "Good night!"

7

Snack Holder Pattern And Recipe Cards
Use with "Snack Attack!" on page 58.

64 ©1999 The Education Center, Inc. • *October Monthly Reproducibles* • Kindergarten • TEC959